ROUTLEDGE LIBRARY EDITIONS:
WOMEN IN ISLAMIC SOCIETIES

Volume 3

THE WOMEN OF THE UNITED ARAB EMIRATES

THE WOMEN OF THE UNITED ARAB EMIRATES

LINDA USRA SOFFAN

LONDON AND NEW YORK

First published in 1980 by Croom Helm Ltd

This edition first published in 2017
by Routledge
2 Park Square, Milton Park, Abingdon, Oxon OX14 4RN

and by Routledge
711 Third Avenue, New York, NY 10017

Routledge is an imprint of the Taylor & Francis Group, an informa business

© 1980 Linda U. Soffan

All rights reserved. No part of this book may be reprinted or reproduced or utilised in any form or by any electronic, mechanical, or other means, now known or hereafter invented, including photocopying and recording, or in any information storage or retrieval system, without permission in writing from the publishers.

Trademark notice: Product or corporate names may be trademarks or registered trademarks, and are used only for identification and explanation without intent to infringe.

British Library Cataloguing in Publication Data
A catalogue record for this book is available from the British Library

ISBN: 978-1-138-20332-7 (Set)
ISBN: 978-1-315-44956-2 (Set) (ebk)
ISBN: 978-1-138-69617-4 (Volume 3) (hbk)
ISBN: 978-1-138-69618-1 (Volume 3) (pbk)
ISBN: 978-1-315-52521-1 (Volume 3) (ebk)

Publisher's Note
The publisher has gone to great lengths to ensure the quality of this reprint but points out that some imperfections in the original copies may be apparent.

Disclaimer
The publisher has made every effort to trace copyright holders and would welcome correspondence from those they have been unable to trace.

The Women of the United Arab Emirates

Linda Usra Soffan

CROOM HELM LONDON

BARNES & NOBLE BOOKS NEW YORK
(a division of Harper & Row Publishers, Inc.)

© 1980 Linda U. Soffan
Croom Helm Ltd, 2-10 St John's Road, London SW11

British Library Cataloguing in Publication Data

Soffan, Linda Usra
  Women of the United Arab Emirates.
  1. Women – United Arab Emirates – Social
  Conditions
  I. Title
  301;41'.2'09535   HQ1731.5
  ISBN 0-7099-0301-4

Published in the USA 1980 by
Harper & Row Publishers, Inc.,
Barnes & Noble Import Division

ISBN 0-06-496396-9
Library of Congress Card Number: 79-57324

To my family, with deepest appreciation and affection

Printed and bound in Great Britain by
Redwood Burn Limited Trowbridge & Esher

CONTENTS

Acknowledgements	
Introduction	9
1. Islamic Law Regarding Women Versus Tribal Traditions and Modern Practices	13
2. Marriage and Family Life in the UAE	28
3. The Role of Education in Raising the Status of the UAE Woman	49
4. The Role of Women in the UAE Economy	66
5. The Role of Governmental and Non-governmental Organizations in Improving the Status of Women in the UAE	84
6. Conclusion	101
Glossary	105
Appendix A: Suras from the Qur'an Relating to Women	106
Appendix B: Total Enrollment of Male/Female UAE Students, 1953-77	113
Current Budget of the UAE Ministry of Education and Youth	114
Educational Stages in the UAE	115
Appendix C: Employment of Local Women in Government Ministries	116
UAE Scholarship Students by Specialization and Class, 1975-6	117
Bibliography	118
Index	126

ACKNOWLEDGEMENTS

This project would not have been possible without the encouragement and assistance of many people and organizations. the UAE Ministries of Culture and Information and Labor and Social Affairs very generously provided the necessary funds for such research as well as contacts with local women's societies, showing not only that they were ready to have such a study done, but, also, that they were willing to consider any recommendations made in the study. I must express my sincere gratitude to 'Abdullah Al-Nuwais, Deputy Minister of Information; 'Abdullah Al-Mazrouie, former Minister of Labor and Social Affairs; and 'Abdullah Abu-Sheehab, Deputy Minister of Labor and Social Affairs.

I would also like to thank Misses Nuhad Kanawaty and Fouda Outa of the local UNICEF office in Abu Dhabi for providing me with useful information on the activities of international organizations in the area.

In the preparation of this study, which is mainly based on my PhD dissertation at the Johns Hopkins School of Advanced International Studies, my adviser, Professor Majid Khadduri, gave me excellent guidance and encouragement at all stages of the project. Dr George Rentz also offered his advice and encouragement. I wish to thank them both.

My thanks are also due to Mary Ann Knotts and Lamin Sise for reading the manuscript in its entirety and offering valuable suggestions.

Had it not been for the cooperation of the female members of the ruling families in the UAE who so warmly received me and made my trip a most memorable one, this project could not have materialized. In particular, I wish to thank Shaykhas Fatima bint Mubarak, Moza bint Hilal, Noura al-Qasimi, Umm 'Ammar, and Mariam Al-Mu'alla.

Finally, my deepest gratitude goes to my husband, Fahim Sultan Al-Qasimi. Had it not been for his unfailing support and encouragement, this project could not have been undertaken in the first place.

As a final note, perhaps the strongest motivating factors in undertaking this research were the writer's years of experience in a first-generation Muslim Arab family in the United States and the numerous courses and readings which gave the writer the impression that Arab women (and those in the Gulf region especially) indeed form a minority which is misunderstood by the Western world. Thus, it is hoped that any information which adds to the existing body of literature will be useful in dispelling a few of the many myths surrounding this special group of Arab women, especially since so much of what is being written today is of a biased, sensational nature.

INTRODUCTION

It was not until the twentieth century that the 'liberation' of women became a topic of concern or interest for large numbers of people throughout the world. Women in the Middle East may have worn a physical veil, but their sisters in the Western world also wore a kind of veil which, though invisible, still kept them in a separate sphere from their menfolk.

Today, it is a popular notion that the degree of social change and development of a society can be measured by the degree of women's emancipation in that society. Depending on where one sets one's focus, Muslim Arab society may appear very advanced or very backward in terms of women's emancipation. However, had this been the same yardstick used to assess Muslim Arab society at the time of the rise of Islam, the Middle East would certainly have been considered most progressive in its treatment of and attitude toward women. As time passed, however, new traditions were created and given a label of Islamic authenticity, when, in reality, they were far from what the Qur'an and Prophet had described as the principles and practices affecting women. In looking at the status and position of Muslim Arab women from one area to the next, the variations in interpretations of Islamic law and traditions are clearly visible.

The Industrial Revolution helped spur positive changes in attitudes toward women in the West. For women in Muslim Arab society, modifications of their status have also come about for many different reasons, at times as a result of a religious reform movement, at other times as an outgrowth of a national liberation movement, or perhaps as a result of the need to use all human resources to bring about rapid development in a certain area.

This study is an examination of the factors which have influenced and continue to affect the position held by women in the United Arab Emirates (UAE) today. A basic premise of this work is that Islamic law has granted women rights and privileges in the spheres of family life, marriage, education and economic pursuits — rights which aim at improving their status in society in general. However, in many cases, because of the interpretations of various religious scholars, influenced by a number of local traditions and social trends, women have not been given the rights due them. Our purpose here is to examine to what

9

10   *Introduction*

extent, if any, UAE society has moved away from strict adherence to these rules and has allowed local tribal traditions regarding women or social trends to take precedence over Islamic law.

Since very little research has previously been done on UAE women, the study relies heavily on field research, most of which was obtained though interviews with various local officials and important private citizens throughout all seven states. To provide a basis for an in-depth study of women's attitudes on certain issues, a standardized set of questions with a wide range of issues was devised. It was assumed that from this broader framework would emerge widely held ideas on specific issues. The results from this questionnaire provided the basis for an examination of the role and status of women as they are related to religious, social and economic factors. The standardized questionnaire helped fulfill the goal of clarifying and correctly defining further issues to be explored. The questionnaire served primarily as an aid in paving the way for the more valuable interviews which were carried out with a select group of women. Therefore, the questionnaire was not the prime focus of the study but rather served as an introduction to the subject matter.

Included among the interviewees were members of the ruling families in Abu Dhabi, 'Ajman, Ras Al-Khaymah, Sharjah and Umm Al-Qaywayn. Other women interviewed were pioneers in the fields of nursing, petroleum engineering, law, broadcasting, social work, education, law enforcement and business. Also interviewed were some of the women of the older generation who had fewer years of formal schooling but whose backgrounds provided invaluable explanatory information on the chain of events which spurred a radical change in lifestyles and attitudes of UAE women in a very short period of time.

The writer also conducted interviews with a group of professionals on employment-related issues. School directresses, social workers, teachers, administrators, nurses, doctors, and women's organization heads made available to the writer a wealth of information crucial to an objective analysis of UAE women.

Chapter 1 examines the position of women in traditional UAE society and the changes they have undergone, and we look at the Muslim view of women and how it evolved. On the basis of the information collected in the field, discussion then moves to the UAE woman as she is within her own environment. Chapter 2 focuses, therefore, on marriage and family life in the UAE and presents an examination of the role of the UAE woman as a family person: as daughter, wife and mother. Here we look at the frequency of child marriages, arranged

Introduction 11

marriages, divorce, remarriage and widowhood, as well as bride-price, polygamy, the socialization process of children and the emergence of the nuclear family in UAE society.

The role of education in improving the status of women is discussed in Chapter 3, and here are explored such topics as women's access to higher education and the services provided to women in school. In Chapter 4 we discuss the role of the UAE woman in the economy and labor force, where work and honor, as well as rights, feature prominently.

Chapter 5 considers the availability of public services to improve the status of women and how successful they have been in reaching these women. The interests of the ruling families in raising the status of women are also discussed here.

In the Conclusion we find that, although local traditions have greatly affected women's status in the past, especially in family matters, Islamic law has been strictly applied to the areas of women's rights to equal educational and employment opportunities, so women's status has been relatively high. With the discovery of oil and the great advantages that accompanied it, the position of UAE women has been further strengthened and will continue to improve in the future.

While the inhabitants of the UAE are divided into the two traditional Arab categories of the *Hadar*, or settled peoples, and the *Bedu*, or nomadic people of the desert, who comprise approximately 10 percent of the population, this study concerns women belonging to the settled population. In reality, however, the differences between the two groups are not always completely obvious because the Bedouins are becoming sedentarized and many of the townspeople have yet to lose all the traits of their Bedouin origins. Thus, while the need for tribal affinity is diminishing today, it does not necessarily mean that tribal traditions or attitudes have also disappeared. Actually, until the wealth brought about by oil, society in the settled communities was only slightly more complex and sophisticated than that of the Bedouins.

The discovery of oil and the wealth that accompanied it brought heretofore unimaginable opportunities and experiences to the people of the Gulf area, but social customs and traditions are always the slowest to change. At present, UAE society and culture is in the midst of a very rapid process of modernization in the fields of social and economic development. The people in the area have undergone a rapid transition from a traditional type of existence where the origins of Arab Bedouin life were predominant to a comparatively modern lifestyle overnight. All of this has had and continues to have profound effects on all mem-

12 *Introduction*

bers of society. Therefore, in attempting to understand the status of women in contemporary UAE society, one must necessarily study the tribal traditions and practices which have long affected, and continue to influence, the rank and status of the UAE woman.

Where fishing and trading were the main occupations before, employment and economic opportunities now seem unlimited. As a consequence, women are being encouraged to participate in this period of growth so that all human resources are fully utilized. In addition, and most importantly, schools have opened up and, for the first time, boys and girls have access to modern education. However, even though nothing is denied either sex in the way of educational and economic pursuits, this does not detract from the social differentiation of men and women. This is, perhaps, the most important reason for studying men and women separately.

1 ISLAMIC LAW REGARDING WOMEN VERSUS TRIBAL TRADITIONS AND MODERN PRACTICES

The Pre-Islamic Position of Women

While much is made of such famous female monarchs as the queen of Sheba and Zenobia of Palmyra, and although a number of poetesses contributed to the great Arabic literary period of the sixth century, those women who are recorded as having held high status seem to be the exception rather than the rule. Although there is some disagreement as to the status of women in pre-Islamic Arabia, it is generally accepted that they held a subordinate position since up to the time of the Prophet Muhammad institutions did not exist which could protect the rights of women. And since so much material in the Qur'an is related to women, it would appear that Qur'anic legislation concerning them aimed at improving the low position which women held at that time.[1]

One reflection of the additudes toward women in the pre-Islamic period is the practice of female infanticide, of which neither the extent nor the reasons are definitely known. While the explanations given by historians are quite varied and range from positive to negative,[2] according to the Qur'an the reasons were poverty and an over-abundance of females since so many men were killed in war.[3]

Among some of the tribes of ancient Arabia, there is evidence of matriarchally organized society and a form of polyandry was practiced in what Robertson Smith described as the *sadica* marriage.[4] The *sadica* marriage resembled the *mut'a* marriage, which also existed at this time, because the *mahr* was paid directly to the bride and not to her guardians. Under the *sadica* arrangement, the woman stayed with her tribe and had the right to dismiss her husband whenever she wished; she was sovereign in the marital relationship.[5]

One hypothesis stated to explain the pre-Islamic Arabian social system is that the society was in transition from a matrilineal to a patrilineal system.[6] Medina is often cited as having a matrilineal social system at this time, but this did not necessarily hold for other parts of Arabia. Most of the evidence designates the patrilineal or *ba'al* marriage as being most prevalent, in which case the woman went to live with her husband. She was completely subject to his authority and he alone had the right of divorce.[7] Marriages did not last long and the men married

13

14 *Islamic Law Regarding Women*

repeatedly.[8] Whether or not polygamy as we now know it existed, there obviously was no stability in a marriage relationship and divorce was common.[9]

The spouse was usually chosen from among a girl's relatives. The decision was left to the girl's parents or guardians and *ibn 'amm* marriages were preferred, although the girl did have the right to refuse the chosen mate. For the female, marriage usually took place at puberty, while marriage for the male could occur at any time, and his age in relation to the bride was not important. The most important criteria in making a suitable match was that the groom be equal to or above the girl in station, for to marry below one's rank would bring dishonor to the bride's tribe.[10] In addition, women had no rights of inheritance or property ownership as even their *mahr* was given to their father or guardian and never to the bride personally, thus leaving women completely dependent and subject to their menfolk.[11]

A final observation is that women of this period enjoyed more social freedom than their post-Islamic sisters and moved freely among their tribesmen, unveiled. It is possible that in the cities there was some veiling, but this was a custom imported from the East and the extent of its practice is not fully known.[12]

Position of Women Under Islamic Law

Islamic law, as laid out in the Qur'an, was, of necessity, rigid and emphatic because of the fact that Arab society was a very conservative and recalcitrant one. There would have been no need for such a legal system had religious and ethical standards been comprehensively applied to all areas of human behaviour, but in regards to the position of women, family life, retaliation, wine drinking, usury and gambling, new standards had to be drawn.[13] Even when Islamic law was introduced by the Prophet, he was aware of the difficulty involved in seeing that the laws were observed. And rightly so, for in a matter of generations the laws concerning women, in particular, were ingeniously changed by Muslim casuists. Too often the Prophet is attacked as having been anti-women, but in examining the Qur'an — which we shall rely on as being the major determinant of the position of women — and *Hadith* (Prophetic traditions) one finds this an unfair accusation. Muhammad not only was aware of women's needs, but also strove to respond to them through legislation.[14]

It is often stated that Islam in general relegates women to a status lower and therefore unequal to that of men. However, in Sura XLIX, verse 13,[15] it is very clearly stated:

Islamic Law Regarding Women

O mankind, we created you all from a male and female, and made you into races and tribes, that you may know one another. Surely the noblest among you in the sight of God is the most God fearing of you.

Here, as in Sura XXXIII, verse 35, race, color and sex are rejected as measures of stratification since only the degree of one's religiosity is important in judging one person as being superior to the next. Otherwise, men and women are considered equal in the eyes of God.

Sura IV, verse 34, is also often used to defend the argument that men and women are not equal, but in stating 'Men are in charge of women, because Allah hath made the one to excel the other, and because they spend of their property (for the support of women)', what is meant is that man is head of the household. The woman is responsible for the upbringing of the children and for all else within the confines of the home, while the man is responsible for what happens outside the house as he is the primary breadwinner.[16] The notion of complementarity emerges here — one stays home because it is easier to tend to the necessary domestic responsibilities, including nursing the children, while the other goes outside the home because it is more convenient for that sex to leave for longer stretches of time. This very much follows the pattern we find in all traditional societies.[17]

A sign of the equality of men and women is seen in the fact that during the Prophet's time women prayed in the mosques but, once seclusion became popular, women were no longer permitted to attend.[18]

The practice of veiling and seclusion were not introduced by Muhammad because he saw women as 'continually giving trouble to man', as some short-sighted Western commentators prefer to explain this phenomenon.[19] Nor was it introduced because it saves the 'naturally unattractive' women from being rejected by men, as an equally myopic Easterner put it.[20] This custom did not even exist in the *Jahiliyah* among tribal society. The Prophet did advise women to cover themselves modestly but this was greatly exaggerated later on. Nor were veiling and segregation of men and women purely Muslim practices, for Christians and Jews in the Middle East also veiled and secluded their women up to the twentieth century.[21] It is believed that veiling was a common practice in ancient Persia and was brought over and adopted by the upper classes in the settled areas of Arabia as a sign of prestige.

It may have been to give his wives a position of honor and dignity, also, that they were veiled, or perhaps Muhammad was convinced of the need for his wives to be secluded later on, after they had allegedly been

16 *Islamic Law Regarding Women*

exposed to insults from various critics of the Prophet.[22] The explanation given for Sura XXXIII, verse 59, is that his wives and followers should cover up so they would not be attacked when out in public.[23] It is said that, prior to Islam, moral codes were lacking and people had a tendency toward immodesty. So, while women are told to be modest in Sura XXIV, verse 31, directly prior to this, in verse 30, men are also similarly advised. Therefore, one sex is not treated any differently from the other in this regard. And when women are told not to display their 'ornaments', this is interpreted to mean the hair, and not the face.

The example set by the Prophet's wives led to the institutionalization of veiling and seclusion and thus both became a sign of prestige. By the end of the eighth century, all women except slaves were completely shut off from the world beyond their private quarters.[24] Thus seclusion became a way of differentiating between slaves and free women. At the same time, within the secluded sector two societies resulted – that of women and that of men. Here it must be stressed that nowhere in the Qur'an is seclusion and veiling of the face mentioned; it was therefore, local customs and tradition which brought these on and preserved them.

Islamic laws pertaining to polygamy are also often misunderstood. As noted earlier, marriage in pre-Islamic Arabia was not known for its longevity and men married repeatedly. As Levy states: 'Before Muhammad, the capacity of the Arab's purse would appear to have provided the only limitation to the number of his wives.'[25] By limiting the number of wives to four (Sura IV:3) it was hoped the position of women would be ameliorated.[26] Equality of treatment and time spent with each was demanded for all, and if this was not possible then only one wife should be taken. Because it was not believed possible to be fair to all, especially in terms of emotional attention, since Muhammad himself is known to have favored 'A'isha above his other wives, polygamy was not recommended.

Although marriage is regarded as a sort of contract between two parties, since no religious ceremony is necessary to make it valid, this does not mean Islam holds marriage lightly. Marriage is encouraged (Sura XXX:21) and rules are laid down as to who might be suitable spouses (Suras IV:20, 25, V:5, XXIV:32). Women are not, for example, forced to marry first cousins, as was the custom in pre-Islamic times, but may marry any man who is a believer (Sura II:221). Furthermore, a sense of responsibility of the husband to the wife is expressed (Sura II:240, IV:5), a factor which is not mentioned in the literature on pre-Islamic women.

Islamic Law Regarding Women 17

An extra-marital relationship by either spouse constitues *zina'* and punishment is equally severe for both women and men (Sura XXIV: 2).

The Qur'an also stipulated that at the time of marriage the dowry was to be given to the bride and not to her family, as was the case prior to Islam (Sura IV:4). This was another gain for women.

Divorce in Islam should be the last resort only after other measures taken have failed to bring about a reconciliation (Sura IV:35). This is not a right accorded to men alone but women, too, can divorce their spouses if just cause is given. A woman can be free if she agrees to give back the *mahr* (Sura II:229) and once this has been done the husband loses any rights over her. Moreover, the Qur'an made it illegal to divorce a wife on a false charge whereby the husband might try to claim some of her property (Sura IV:20).[27] Men are urged to 'keep their women in kindness or to release them in kindness' (Sura II:231) as failing to do so may be in opposition to the will of God (Sura IV:19).

Since, prior to Islam, women had no rights of inheritance or property ownership (unless a woman outlived all her male relatives, as supposedly was the case with Khadija, Muhammad's first wife), Qur'anic legislation referring to this was considered a great improvement in women's status (Sura IV:7 and 32).[28] All are encouraged to make out wills (Sura II:177) and the female's right to bequeath is guaranteed in Sura IV:12. Any changes since then result from a neglect of Muslim inheritance laws concerning women.[29]

Infanticide was also made illegal by Qur'anic legislation (Suras VI: 151, XXVII:31), so the status of children, and of females especially, was shifted by Islam. Suras referring to paternity, support, adoption and inheritance also did much to raise the status of children.[30]

Undeniably, Islam did not provide a solution to every problem plaguing women at that time, but Muhammad did succeed in making great progress in the elevation of their status. What has been discussed in this section are those parts of Qur'anic legislation which helped in this endeavor. But, as we said earlier, social attitudes and traditions are always the hardest and slowest to change; and we find this to be the case especially in tribal society.

Position of Women in Arab Tribal Society

As Islam spread, that group which proved most resistant to the changes demanded by the new religion consisted of the Arab Bedouins, mainly because of their dedication to custom and tradition.[31]

The Prophet himself feared the attachment held by the Bedouins to their forefathers, and throughout the Qur'an reference is made to the

18   *Islamic Law Regarding Women*

unruliness of the Bedouins.[32] Transferring loyalty and devotion from the clan or tribe to one God was difficult for them to accept; especially since many of the laws sent by Allah were in opposition to the traditions of their ancestors. But once the tribes were won over and Islam prevailed, the tribesmen became staunch supporters of their new religion.

Although the inhabitants of the Arabian Peninsula were the instruments through which Islam began its conquest of the Eastern world,[33] they were destined eventually to retreat from that prospering society into their tribal society. Therefore, since this part of the peninsula was barely touched by foreign influence until the twentieth century, it was easy for Arab tribal society to maintain its own way of life. In retrospect, the tribesmen's lifestyle changed very little after the rise of Islam,[34] and their practice of the religious tenets lacked conviction.[35] It was for the very reason that the Arab tribes were still living in ignorance of Islam and the *shari'a* that Muhammad Ibn 'Abd Al-Wahhab called for a religious revival in the mid-eighteenth century.[36]

Tribal society, as it existed and continues to exist among the nomadic and settled Bedouins of the Arabian Peninsula, consists of families linked by patrilineal ties.[37] The heads of these families had great prestige and were chosen according to seniority, lineage and their reputation for wisdom. Their duties centered around family ties, 'blood ransom' or vengeance, and hospitality.[38]

In Arab society in general, whether tribal or familial, status is something ascribed and not achieved, and the determining factor here is honor. Within both systems, honor is the criterion of value judgment. Either you do or you do not have honor; it is easy to lose and hard to win back. The Bedouin, like his sedentary kinsman, is constantly preoccupied with maintaining and preserving honor, and, in tribal and family custom, the chastity of the woman is the embodiment of the honor of the family.[39] Perhaps it was with this awareness that Harold Dickson was prompted to declare: 'True it is that you can make a Badawin man or woman do pretty well anything in this world except ... sacrifice his or her honor, by the offer of money.'[40]

The woman is the repository of moral deeds in her family, thus she can destroy the honor of the family. She carries her family honor with her even after marriage and she continues to represent her family through her modesty. A woman's male descendents inherit their honor from her and, therefore, a woman is always closest to her brothers and her sons as it is through her that their honor is determined and maintained and, should she commit a major wrong, it is they who must

Islamic Law Regarding Women

19

punish her.[41]

The period from puberty until the time of marriage is a most uneasy one for the family of a girl. Because they fear for their honor, the family arranges for the marriage of the daughter as soon as possible. For this reason, when the girl reaches puberty, she dons the veil and stays within the female quarters. The nomadic woman enjoys a bit more social freedom than her sisters in the towns and villages only because of her rigorous lifestyle, which entails everything from cooking, cleaning and weaving, to tending the livestock.

Because of the immense responsibility women hold, it is understandable why men respect and, at the same time, fear women so much. By their seclusion, whether in the special quarters of the tent or the house, women do not come in contact with any person except the closest of relatives and the family never risks loss of honor. In what space is allotted to tribal women in the older narratives describing life in Arabia, the writers all point out how women are excluded from any male company outside their immediate family and several dwell on the consequences should a woman be merely suspected of committing a dishonorable act.[42]

In tribal society, there remains a preference for first-cousin marriages (*ibn 'amm*) and the bride-price more often than not goes to the bride and not to the bride's family. However, so long as marriage remains within the clan, the *mahr* is not very high and marriage for the purpose of maintaining old or acquiring new tribal loyalties may be a reason for overlooking the *mahr* altogether and demanding it only if relationships break down.[43] When the bride does receive the *mahr* for her personal use, she uses it to purchase gold, which serves as a form of security should she later have to support herself.

Although divorce and remarriage are common in tribal society, rarely can a man afford to keep more than one wife at a time unless he is a *shaykh* and is thereby trying to form political alliances by marrying into as many families as possible.[44] There is no stigma attached to divorce and it is not unusual for a woman to marry several times in her life, especially if she is from a good family or renowned for her beauty. As long as she has a living son, however, the chances of divorce are slimmer as the most common causes are barrenness or the lack of male heirs.[45] Up to the time when a woman produces a male heir, her position as wife may remain unstable.

Should the woman herself request a divorce, it is often easier for the Bedouin wife than for her other Arab sisters. The Bedouin woman only packs her bags and returns to her family (which usually is not too far

20   *Islamic Law Regarding Women*

away if she is married to a cousin). The husband can either try to woo her back through gifts or give her a divorce. If the woman is intent on the latter, rather than risk humiliation in the eyes of the menfolk, the husband will usually grant the divorce, in which case the wife is expected to return the *mahr*. In any case, once divorced, the woman always returns to her own family, where she remains until remarriage or the end of her life.

It is customary for a woman to marry within or above her rank, but never lower. Although Islam is opposed to favoring one man over another on the basis of lineage, this is a tribal custom.[46] Problems may exist for women of the ruling families as here it is unusual for daughters to be married outside the family, even to members of other ruling families. There are exceptions to the rule,[47] and occasionally a daughter may marry outside the tribe, but if a suitable mate is not found the only choice is spinsterhood.

Once Islam overcame the original opposition of the Arabs, it became an integral part of tribal society, thereafter viewed as a sacred tradition passed down from their forefathers. And in matters relating to the family, the religious laws are closely observed.[48] Male and female are taught the Qur'an, sometimes even in a co-ed atmosphere if only one instructor is available.[49] It is not unusual for the women to be more devout than the men, though both perform the ceremonial prayers five times a day.[50] Nor is it unusual for women to become more well read than men; once having mastered the Qur'an, the next step is the *Hadith* and then poetry.[51]

Over the centuries, the status of women in tribal society has changed little, if at all. The matrilineal period, for however long it existed, if in fact it did exist in more than a few special cases, came and went, and now women's position is determined by patrilineage. In some respects, the treatment of women is influenced by the laws set down by Islam, but equality of the sexes has not been realized in tribal practices. Here the fault lies not in Islam but in the difficulty of incorporating such a radical idea into tribal customs which constitute an obstacle to change. However, with modernization, which brings economic and social change, tribal practices and customs have of necessity begun to break down in the Arabian Gulf, just as they have already dissipated in other parts of the Arab world.

The Impact of Modernization on the Position of Arab Women

Modernization means different things to different people or groups thereof. For those Arab women who have been experiencing change for

Islamic Law Regarding Women 21

the past 50 years or so, 'modernization' has meant a change in the basic social structure from large, extended families to small, nuclear families; an opportunity for formal education for the first time; employment opportunities in the labor market in a variety of occupations and a new-found awareness of the world around them through new systems of communication (i.e., television, radio, newspapers and modern forms of transportation).

For the Arab women in those countries which had been under Eastern, then Western, occupation for centuries, the demand for change in their status coincided with the rise of nationalism in the various Muslim countries and the need to catch up with the West after centuries of social and economic stagnation. The causes of nationalism and feminism were thus brought together in Egypt and Palestine, as well as in the non-Arab Muslim states of India, Iran and Turkey.[52] In the other Arab countries, it took a bit longer for change to come about because of varying social and political circumstances, but slowly the powerful combination of nationalist and feminist forces brought change to Lebanese, Syrian, Iraqi and Jordanian women, as well as to women thoughout North Africa. In the case of Algeria and Palestine women actually fought side by side with men in the national liberation struggle, and Palestinian women continue to do so today. This does not necessarily assure them equal status, but their position has improved greatly.[53]

Though the circumstances varied from country to country, the veil slowly came off, sometimes as a result of several prominent women taking the initiative or after decades of preaching by responsible male leaders.

As long as women were illiterate, it did not matter that they had rights. They were not capable of taking advantage of them as they were probably unaware of their existence. But growing acceptance of women's rights to equal educational opportunities has significantly changed the situation. The success of the reformers and feminists in this sphere led to a whole series of changes for women.

As long as women remained illiterate, there were not many objections to seclusion; but literacy opened up a new world for them with new desires and perspectives that could not be satisfied if they were confined to the *harem*. That is not to say that all women were in favor of greater liberty from the start. On the contrary, many were quite content to stay within the *harem*, and the idea of dropping the veil was repugnant. However, once the notion of education became firmly rooted, as noted by Nadia Youssef, 'Access to educational power sup-

22 *Islamic Law Regarding Women*

planted women's exclusive involvement in domestic affairs and motherhood which was previously the only source of their self-identity, justification for existence and influence.'[54]

The pursuit of secondary or university education has, in many cases, delayed marriages. Furthermore, women's perspectives change and they no longer only wish to become mothers and housewives; they also want to have careers. Therefore, higher education affects the number of children they bear and it affects their desire to seek employment and become economically independent.[55]

The proportion of women employed in the modern economic sector is low throughout the Middle East and many of them still work in the pre-industrial sector.[56] However, because of the growing need for women to contribute to national development, more and more women are being welcomed into the modern skilled sectors and at higher levels. Up to the present time, however, those women who are in the professions are concentrated in teaching and nursing and hold very few positions in clerical occupations, factories and business — all of which remain male strongholds.[57]

Programs for population control have been widely established by various governments and have enjoyed a high degree of acceptance, even in the rural areas.[58] With higher life expectancy and the increased financial strains associated with raising large families, women are increasingly opting for smaller families. Of course, this does not hold true for the entire Arab world, as some countries (the oil-rich states especially) are very much in need of a population increase, and couples are provided with monetary incentives to have larger families. In the poorer, over-crowded countries, however, birth control is a strongly supported government policy.

Through greater opportunities to travel and the introduction of television and radio in the Middle East, larger numbers of people became aware of the differences from, and greater comforts afforded to, individuals in the West, women especially. The West was seen as the model for change in the Middle East, not only for women's status but also for the structure of the family. Since the early 1900s, with women sharing more of the household expenses after taking on jobs outside the home, it has become economically feasible for a young couple to live on their own in a separate home from their parents, as is the custom in the West.[59] Thus, the typical extended family has been replaced by the nuclear family and, although the patriarchal family is still the basis of Arab society, the hallowed authority of the father has to a degree been undermined.[60]

Islamic Law Regarding Women

In addition, young men and women are increasingly unhappy with the former system of accepting an arranged spouse; rather, the modern male or female wants at least to meet and speak with the prospective bride or groom beforehand. Since their lives will be more private, not being exposed to the watchful eye of the extended family, compatability is a prerequisite to a successful marriage. In this way, divorce and polygamy pose less of a threat because the couple have had a chance fairly to determine whether they will be happy together through having met beforehand. And with females out of seclusion, the chances of their meeting a suitable mate increase.[61]

Many government heads have taken more than a passive interest in women's emancipation and outrightly encouraged females to play a more creative role in the modernization of their country.[62] In addition, participation of women in political life has increased and some women have even been awarded cabinet seats (Egypt, Iraq and Sudan).[63]

The reaction of men to these changes ranges from fear to pleasure. They fear that the liberation of their women will result in an adoption of too many undesirable Western characteristics.[64] At the same time, while they are content with less educated wives, they do want to see their daughters educated and are pleased that this opportunity is now available. However, the more educated the man, the more aware he is of the ideals of sexual equality and the more likely it is that he will want an equally well-educated wife.[65]

Along with new opportunities, modernization has also brought an equal share of anxiety and unhappiness. Among the problems women in the Arab Muslim World have been experiencing since the end of veiling and seclusion are the reconciliation of old ways in family relationships to the new and the combining of the good from the West with the good from the East.

In retrospect, Arab women have indeed come a long, long way. Their progress has been slow and not always steady, but this is to be expected; nor have women throughout the region progressed uniformly because of the unique political and economic history of each area.

The Earl of Cromer was being more than a little hard on Islam when he blamed the social ills of its followers on the low status of women;[66] and he seems to have overlooked the fact that significant changes in the status of women in his own country did not come about until after the Industrial Revolution. Indeed, Western women have yet to be completely liberated. But the point was well made that Muslim Arab women had a way to go and — a fact that is often neglected — so did Muslim Arab men. In all fairness, they were not much better off than

24 *Islamic Law Regarding Women*

the women for, as the women were subjects of their male kinfolk, so the men were subjects of their colonizers. Before men could liberate women, they had to liberate themselves.

Women and Modernization in the Arabian Gulf

Since the Arabian Gulf area remained almost completely untouched by Western influences until the twentieth century, women and men of this area have continued to live by many of their primarily tribal traditions and customs up to the present time. And if the Muslim world in general was in relative decline after the fourteenth century, the Gulf area has been in decline even longer, as it remained in isolation from the West until the Portuguese invasion in the sixteenth century,[67] and had only limited contact with its Eastern neighbors until recent time.

Except for the few desert romanticists or adventurers who explored the area and later recorded their recollections, information on the Arabian Gulf remained scanty. It is during the sixteenth century that the recorded modern history of the Arabian Gulf begins,[68] and discussion of women is rare and unsatisfactory. With the exception of some recent studies on women in Kuwayt, Bahrayn and Saudi Arabia, little data has been collected on women in the Lower Gulf area in general, and the area now known as the United Arab Emirates, in particular.

Among the reasons for this paucity of information is that most of these early travelers and explorers who went into the area were men, and the possibility of their meeting any local women, not to mention studying them, was slight. Even today, a woman may venture into the area, but, unless she is accompanied by a male or has a male sponsor, she will also experience difficulties in meeting local women.

Given the unique social position of women in this area, a study of the position of women in the light of Islamic laws and modernization and their attitudes to their lifestyle and environment was undertaken. Through interviews and data collected from UAE women of various backgrounds, such factors as forms of marriage, extent of polygamy and divorce, women's access to educational institutions, and the availability of economic opportunities were examined in the hope that the status of women in the United Arab Emirates could be fairly determined.

Notes

1. Joseph Schacht, 'Pre-Islamic Background and Early Development of Juris-

Islamic Law Regarding Women

prudence' in M. Khadduri and H. Liebesny (eds), *Law in the Middle East* (Middle East Institute, Washington, DC, 1955), p. 28.

2. See, for example, Nabia Abbott, 'Women' in Ruth N. Anshen (ed.), *Mid-East: World Center Yesterday, Today and Tomorrow* (Harper and Brothers, New York, 1956), pp. 196-7. Also, Ilse Lichenstader as quoted in Wendell Phillips, *Unknown Oman* (David McKay, New York, 1968), p. 129. Also see Reuben Levy, *The Social Structure of Islam* (Cambridge University Press, London, 1971), pp. 91-2.

3. *The Glorious Koran*, translated by Marmaduke Pickthall (SUNY, Albany, 1976), Sura XVII, verse 31. (See Appendix A.)

4. W. Robertson Smith, *Kinship and Marriage in Early Arabia* (Cambridge University Press, Cambridge, 1939), pp. 92-4.

5. Ibid., p. 80.

6. Montgomery Watt, *Muhammad: Prophet and Statesman* (Oxford University Press, Oxford, 1969), pp. 151-4.

7. Smith, *Kinship and Marriage*, p. 92.

8. Arthur Jeffery, 'The Family in Islam' in Ruth N. Anshen (ed.), *The Family: Its Function and Destiny* (Harper and Brothers, New York, 1949), pp. 58-9.

9. Gertrude Stern, *Marriage in Early Islam* (The Royal Asiatic Society, London, 1939), p. 70.

10. Jeffery, 'The Family in Islam', pp. 45-7.

11. Levy, *Social Structure of Islam*, pp. 95-8.

12. Jeffery, 'The Family in Islam', pp. 56-7.

13. Schacht, 'Pre-Islamic Background and Early Development of Jurisprudence', pp. 28-33.

14. Hamilton Gibb, *Mohammadanism* (Oxford University Press, Oxford, 1970), pp. 22-3.

15. For all references to the Qur'an, see Appendix A.

16. Muhammed Abdul-Rauf, *The Islamic View of Women and the Family* (Robert Speller and Sons, New York, 1977), pp. 65-7.

17. E. Boserup, *Women's Role in Economic Development* (Allen and Unwin, London, 1970).

18. R.A. and E.W. Fernea, 'Variation in Religious Observance Among Islamic Women' in Nikkie Keddie (ed.), *Scholars, Saints and Sufis* (University Press, Berkeley, California, 1972), pp. 385-6.

19. Vern L. Bullough, *The Subordinate Sex* (University of Illinois Press, Urbana, Illinois, 1973), p. 137.

20. Hajji Shaykh Yusuf, 'In Defense of the Veil' in B. Rivlin and J. Szyliowicz (eds), *The Contemporary Middle East* (Random House, New York, 1965), pp. 355-9.

21. Raphael Patai, *Golden River to Golden Road* (University of Pennsylvania Press, Philadelphia, 1967), p. 117. Gertrude Bell also made note of the veiling and seclusion of Christian women in one of her letters in *The Letters of Gertrude Bell*, selected and edited by Lady Bell (Ernest Benn, London, 1927), vol. 1, p. 181.

22. E. Fernea and B.Q. Bezirgan, *Middle Eastern Muslim Women Speak* (University of Texas Press, Austin, Texas, 1977), pp. 29-30.

23. Jeffery, 'The Family in Islam', p. 57.

24. Gustave E. Von Grunebaum, *Medieval Islam* (University of Chicago Press, Chicago, 1969), p. 175.

25. Levy, *Social Structure of Islam*, p. 100.

26. Charles W. Churchill, 'The Arab World' in Raphael Patai (ed.), *Women in the Modern World* (Free Press, New York, 1967), p. 108.

27. Levy, *Social Structure of Islam*, p. 97.

28. Ibid., pp. 95-8.

26   Islamic Law Regarding Women

29. Gabriel Baer, *Population and Society in the Arab East* (Praeger, New York, 1964), p. 40.

30. See Jeffery, 'The Family in Islam', pp. 63-70.

31. Schacht, 'Pre-Islamic Background and Early Development of Jurisprudence', p. 34.

32. For examples, see Suras IX:97, 120, XLVIII:16.

33. For the various interpretations of the role of the Bedouins of Arabia in assisting with the expansion of Islam, see Carl Becker, 'The Expansion of the Saracens', Chs XI and XII in *The Cambridge Medieval History*, vol. II, pp. 328-90. In addition, see Montgomery Watt, *Muhammad: Prophet and Statesman* (Oxford University Press, Oxford, 1969); and Barbara Aswad, 'Social and Ecological Aspects In the Formation of Islam' in Louise Sweet (ed.), *Peoples and Cultures of the Middle East*, vol. 1 (The Natural History Press, Garden City, New York, 1970), pp. 53-74.

34. Joel Carmichael, *The Shaping of the Arabs: A Study in Ethnic Identity* (Macmillan, London, 1967), p. 35.

35. Philip Hitti, *History of the Arabs* (St Martins, London, 1970), p. 26.

36. R. Bayly Winder, *Saudi Arabia in the 19th Century* (Macmillan, London, 1965).

37. Kazem el-Daghestani, 'The Evolution of the Muslim Family in the Middle Eastern Countries' in Rivlin and Szyliowicz (eds), *Contemporary Middle East* (Random House, New York, 1965), p. 345.

38. Majid Khadduri, *War and Peace in the Law of Islam* (Johns Hopkins Press, Baltimore, Maryland, 1955), p. 21.

39. Fernea and Bezirgan, *Muslim Women Speak*, pp. xix-xx.

40. Harold Dickson, *The Arab of the Desert* (Allen and Unwin, London, 1949), p. 56.

41. For an in-depth study of honor and shame, see J.G. Peristiany, *Honor and Shame: The Values of Mediterranean Society* (University of Chicago Press, Illinois, 1974).

42. Charles Doughty, *Travels in Arabia Deserta*, vol. I and II (Cambridge University Press, Cambridge, 1921), pp. 141-2, 377; Harold Dickson, *Arab of the Desert*, pp. 56-79, 148; Wilfred Thesiger, *Arabian Sands* (E.P. Dutton, New York, 1959), pp. 177-9, 252-3; Wendell Phillips, *Unknown Oman* (David McKay, New York, 1969), pp. 128-46; Elizabeth Fernea, *Guests of the Sheikh* (Doubleday, New York, 1965), pp. 256-66.

43. William Goode, 'Changing Family Patterns in Arabic Islam' in *World Revolution and Family Patterns* (Free Press, New York, 1963), p. 93.

44. Ibid., p. 102. It might be noted that this was a primary reason for the Prophet having married so many women; and, up to the formation of states, marriage for the purpose of forming political alliances remained a common practice in the Gulf.

45. Ibid., pp. 112, 140. Also, P.A. Lienhardt, 'Some Social Aspects of the Trucial States' in Derek Hopwood (ed.), *The Arabian Peninsula* (Rowman and Littlefield, New Jersey, 1972), p. 223; Harold Dickson, *Arab of the Desert*, pp. 143-4.

46. Gabriel Baer, *Population and Society*, p. 63.

47. Dickson, *Arab of the Desert*, p. 143.

48. As Rupert Hay points out in *The Persian Gulf States*, pp. 114-16, it is only in non-family-related matters that the shaykh administers his 'palm-tree' justice.

49. As related to the present writer by more than a few older women, the girls and boys may sit separately, but both are given lessons. Doughty, *Travels in Arabia Deserta*, p. 442 also makes note of this.

Islamic Law Regarding Women   27

50. Donald Cole makes this observation in his study of the Al-Murrah tribe in *Nomads of the Nomads: The Al-Murrah Bedouin of the Empty Quarter* (Aldine, Chicago, 1975), Ch. 6. Also, Dickson, *Arab of the Desert*, pp. 56-7, and Lienhardt, 'Social Aspects of Trucial States', pp. 220-1, note this, as well as Richard Sanger in *Arabian Peninsula* (Books for Libraries, New York, 1954), p. 95.

51. Freya Stark, *The Southern Gates of Arabia* (E.P. Dutton, New York, 1945), p. 140. And Nabia Abbott, 'Women', pp. 202-3.

52. Ruth Woodsmall, *Muslim Women Enter a New World* (Middle East Institute, Washington, DC, 1936), pp. 362-72.

53. David C. Gordon, *Women of Algeria – An Essay on Change*, Harvard University, Cambridge, Mass., 1968), pp. 50-83. Judith Stiehm, 'Algerian Women: Honor, Survival, and Islamic Socialism' in L.B. Iglitzin and R. Ross (eds), *Women in the World: A Comparative Study* (Clio Books, Santa Barbara, California, 1976), pp. 229-41.

54. Nadia Youssef, 'Women in the Muslim World' in Iglitzen and Ross (eds), *Women in the World: A Comparative Study* (Clio Books, Santa Barbara, California, 1976), p. 208.

55. Ibid., p. 208.

56. Fatima Mernissi, 'The Moslem World: Women Excluded from Development' in Irene Tinker and Michele Bramsen (eds), *Women and World Development* (Overseas Development Council, Washington, 1976), pp. 38-9. Also, Khadija Nouacer, 'The Changing Status of Women and the Employment of Women in Morocco' in *International Social Science Journal*, vol. 14, no. 1 (1962), pp. 124-9; and *UNESCO*, 'Report on the Relationship Between Educational Opportunities for Women' (Paris, July 1975), pp. 75-82.

57. Nadia Youssef, *Women and Work in Developing Societies*, Population Monograph Series no. 15 (University of California, Berkeley, 1974), pp. 22-62.

58. For an example of this, see Perdita Houston, *Message from the Village* (Epoch Foundation, New York, 1978), pp. 30-62. Also, Nadia Youssef, 'Women in the Muslim World', pp. 211-12.

59. Jacques Berque, *The Arabs: Their History and Future* (Praeger, New York, 1964), p. 188.

60. Peter Mansfield, *The Arabs* (Penguin Books, London, 1977), pp. 545-6.

61. Morroe Berger, *The Arab World* (Doubleday, New York, 1964), pp. 124-5.

62. Habib Bourguiba, 'A New Role for Women' in Rivlin and Szyliowicz (eds), *Contemporary Middle East* (Random House, New York, 1965), pp. 352-5. Also, Roger Le Tournean, Maurice Flory, Rene Duchoc, 'Revolution in the Maghreb' in P.J. Vatikiotis (ed.), *Revolution in the Middle East* (Allen and Unwin, London, 1972), pp. 73-119. In addition, see Ann Dearden (ed.), *Arab Women*, Report no. 27 (Minority Rights Group, London, 1976), pp. 5, 9-12, 15; and Fred Halliday, *Arabia Without Sultans* (Vintage, New York, 1975), pp. 242, 251-5.

63. Gabriel Baer, *Population and Society*, p. 57.

64. Fatima Mernissi, *Beyond the Veil* (Shenkman, Cambridge, Mass., 1975), p. 101.

65. Morroe Berger, *The Arab World* (Doubleday, New York, 1964), pp. 133-4.

66. Earl of Cromer, *Modern Egypt* (Macmillan and Co., London, 1908), pp. 134-5.

67. Donald Hawley, *The Trucial States* (Twayne, New York, 1971), pp. 68-79.

68. Husain Albaharna, *The Arabian Gulf States: Their Legal and Political Status and Their International Problems* (Librairie Du Liban, Beirut, 1975), p. 5.

2 MARRIAGE AND FAMILY LIFE IN THE UAE

The Practice in the UAE of Islamic Legal Norms Relating to Marriage and Family Life

Unlike some of its sister Arab States which have revised Islamic marriage and family laws (such as restrictions on minimum age at time of marriage and the abolition of the unrestrained right of repudiation), the Islamic laws relating to marriage and family are still fully intact in the UAE.[1] Therefore, since there is general conformity of practice with these laws, there will be no need for much reform.

Marriage and family law, as derived from the Qur'an, was, indeed, revolutionary at the time when it was revealed. Under Islam, for a marriage to be considered valid, no religious or ceremonial rites are necessary. Instead, a marriage contract is drawn up, this being either oral or written, consisting of an offer by the man and an acceptance by the woman, before a minimum of two witnesses. The contract must not stipulate that it is of limited duration, and it must be made public.[2] Then, once all the necessary conditions are met, such as payment of the dowry, the contract is completed.

Often, the bride herself does not participate in the actual arrangement of the contract. The idea of a *wali*, or marriage-guardian, to speak for the bride goes back to pre-Islamic times, when the *mahr* was paid to the bride's father and not to her personally. The *wali's* position is not mentioned in the Qur'an, and whether or not the Prophet sanctioned it cannot be determined by the literature. However, it is reported that in several instances the Prophet himself was offered the hand in marriage of young women, by the women themselves.[3] All four legal schools recognize the existence and need for a *wali*, but they agree that he does not have absolute control over the bride's decision to marry, and, therefore, a marriage contract without the bride's consent is considered invalid.[4]

Marriage to persons with whom the bride or groom shares a special relationship is also forbidden by Qur'anic law. Various blood kin are considered prohibited, as are persons with certain ties through marriage or 'milk'[5] relationships.

Remarriage is delayed for reasons of death or divorce of the husband, and the widowed woman must wait four months and ten days before remarrying, while the divorced woman has a three-month

Marriage and Family Life in the UAE 29

waiting period.

Although the Qur'an does not specify that a woman must marry a Muslim man only, all four schools specify that marriage to a non-Muslim is not valid unless the husband converts to Islam. The Muslim man, on the other hand, is free to marry any follower of a revealed religion (i.e., Islam, Judaism or Christianity).

The institution of polygamy is probably one of the most controversial issues in Islam. Whether or not it was the purpose of Islam to encourage polygamy by permitting up to four wives at a time is still not known. However, the general consensus seems to be that, as stated by Majid Khadduri, 'The ultimate purpose of Qur'anic marriage law, ...was to legitimate monogamy rather than to endorse polygamy'.[6]

In the choosing of a spouse, determinants of suitability are not stated in Qur'anic law and the existence of *Hadith* pertaining to this is disputed by some legal schools. In general, however, it is accepted that a woman must marry a man of equal 'station', and here the important considerations are: religious affiliation (he must be a Muslim), piety, free status, financial suitability and occupation.[7]

The *mahr* must be paid by the husband to the bride, and she is free to use this as she pleases. It is not necessary to pay the full amount at the time of marriage, and all or part of it can be deferred, depending on the agreement of the concerned parties. No contract is valid without a bride-price, and, when one is not stated, the *mahr* of a woman of similar status is paid.[8]

The wife has no financial duties in the marriage, and any property she acquires throughout her lifetime is hers alone to manage. Should a husband not be able to support his wife in the manner to which she is accustomed, most legal schools would agree that she is free to divorce him.

Termination of the marriage contract, an act strongly opposed by Islam, is justifiable only after all attempts at reconciliation have failed. At that point, divorce by the husband occurs through his making an oral declaration to the wife that the marriage is terminated. A woman, however, cannot secure a divorce from her husband without the intervention of a *qadi*, unless the power to do so is provided in the marriage contract or the wife is thus empowered by her husband at some point in the marriage.[9]

The rights of children are also fully and carefully delineated in Islam. They, too, are totally dependent on the father for support, although the mother is responsible for their early upbringing (up to age seven for a boy and age nine for a girl). On reaching puberty, the male child is

30 *Marriage and Family Life in the UAE*

considered independent and free to act and move as he pleases. The female child, however, remains under the guardianship of her father or other male relative until the time she marries, or until she is old enough to be considered capable of attending to her own affairs.[10]

The wealth brought about by oil has, in most cases, strengthened the position of women in the UAE with respect to marriage and family law, although, in general, women in tribal societies have traditionally held a stronger position than that of their peasant or urban Arab sisters. An example of this is the fact that men of this area have long leaned toward monogamy, a tendency especially influenced by economic reasons. Although they can afford more than one wife, they continue to be monogamous as a matter of principle and because monogamy is characterized as a trait of 'modern' countries, and they wish to be considered a modernizing people. There are some men who exercise their right of polygamy only to show their peers they can afford many wives, and remarry as often as possible. This is the exception rather than the rule here. The right of repudiation, which long posed a fear for other Arab women, has never caused great anxiety in the UAE, as divorce in tribal society is usually for reasons of barrenness or incompatibility, and divorce bears no stigma. The practice of cousin marriages, though not of Islamic legal origin, has continued to be the best method for deciding on a match for a girl, but even this is changing and women are having a greater say in choosing a spouse.

In general, marriage and raising a family have been and continue to be the prime goals for every girl. In this there is full conformity with Islam, as the religion encourages marriage. It is only when the parents or husband take advantage of this institution, through forced early marriage, marriage without the girl's consent, or repudiation without just cause, for example, that conflict with the law arises.

Selection of the Marriage Partner in the UAE

Marriage is by arrangement, and the bride, who often does not meet the groom before the wedding night, has little if any say in the decision. Although the right to refuse a match exists, rarely is this exercised, as young girls are not in a position to question the arrangement. In a society where children are conditioned from infancy that this is to be their fate, there was little reason to question it, especially since there were no alternatives, such as have only recently become available. In all but a very small minority of the women interviewed, marriages were arranged by the parents, and the approval of the girl was not solicited. However, the majority of these women would prefer that their own

Marriage and Family Life in the UAE 31

daughters be allowed a greater say in this important decision, although the father's opinion would still carry great weight.[11]

There is preference for first-cousin marriages, be they paternal or maternal first cousins,[12] although it is not unusual for marriages to be arranged outside the family circle. As long as the groom is of equal or better status than the bride, there is no problem. The most important factors taken into consideration when arranging marriage for one's daughter is that her intended spouse be equal to her in birth (being of pure Arab stock), religion, degree of freedom and wealth or occupation.[13] As long as the girl marries within the family, the question of inferiority does not arise.

In the case of ruling families, *shaykhs'* daughters are married to other *shaykhs'* sons, and always within the same family, so as to keep the unit together. It is rare for the daughter of one ruling family to marry the son of another ruling family. When that is the only choice available to a girl, she will often remain unmarried, although spinsterhood is not at all encouraged by Islam. It is very common for *shaykhs'* sons to marry daughters of wealthy, well-established families who gained importance and respect through their business success before the development of oil wealth. Through intermarriage, the men of these families grew to have close ties; the men of the leading families continue to hold great prestige in the eyes of the *shaykhs* today, and some have been offered high government positions.

Marriages of *shaykhs* to Bedouin women are also common. Traditionally, this was a way of bringing more tribes over to one's side, when the need for such alliances existed. It is not unusual to hear of older *shaykhs* who married twenty or thirty times to secure political support among the Bedouin, although this is not a common occurrence today. Regardless of the duration of the marriage, the woman gains prestige for having married a *shaykh*, and remarriage is not a problem for her.

The procedures followed in arranging a traditional marriage are that, when a man is ready for marriage, he expresses his intentions to his family. Then the womenfolk go about trying to select a suitable spouse. Since all of the eligible girls in the area are known to them, the man's mother and sisters are responsible for describing each girl to him, and the final decision is his. Of course, their personal opinion is all that he can rely on since there is no chance of his meeting a potential spouse personally. Although there is nothing in the Qur'an which states the prospective bride and groom cannot meet before marriage, they are not given this opportunity. Even today, after the engagement and the contract has been signed, a girl may speak with the prospective groom on

32 *Marriage and Family Life in the UAE*

the telephone or exchange letters and photos, but rarely do they meet. The only opportunity for pre-marital acquaintance would have occurred when, or if, they were childhood playmates, or if they are related. Because the mother and sisters know their female relatives best, it is likely that they will favor eligible girls within this circle. It is not unusual for cousins to be told from childhood that they are 'perfectly suited' for each other and will marry when the time is proper. The mother, especially, will try to convince the son that a maternal cousin is most suitable, and very often the son will follow her wishes. Very often the father, too, will suggest a possible bride, but the son is not forced to marry anyone in particular. If it is the father who is paying the *mahr* for his son, his opinion admittedly carries great weight, but the decision is, in the final analysis, the son's alone.

Once the bride is chosen, the man sends one or two women, usually his mother and an older sister, to speak with her mother. The girl's mother, in turn, informs her husband of the proposal. The girl's father then decides whether to accept or reject the offer after he has had time to reflect on the prospective groom's background. In some cases, the man himself approaches the girl's family. First he will speak with her mother, and if there is a possibility of a match he is then advised to meet with her father. In other instances, the man and his father will approach the girl's father, in which case no women are involved in the process. This often occurs if the man is related to the family or knows them very well.

If the girl's father is not living and she has no older brother, only her mother is approached, and the mother alone makes the final decision. Her male guardian, most likely a paternal uncle, is the one to sign the contract, but his role is often a marginal one, especially if strong ties have not been maintained with the paternal relatives throughout the girl's life. If the girl's parents are divorced, the man goes directly to her father to make the proposal and, again, the womenfolk need not be consulted or involved.

In all these cases, the girl may or may not be informed of the marriage proposal until shortly before the wedding. Of course today this is slowly changing, and the girl's feelings are increasingly being taken into consideration. Also, as will be discussed later, the procedures differ somewhat for a divorced or widowed woman whose hand in marriage is being sought. In these arrangements, the women always have some say.

Once a girl reaches puberty, she dons the *burqu'* and *'abayah* and is thereafter confined to the *harem*. She is then considered eligible for marriage. Traditionally, the age of the groom was not important, and

Marriage and Family Life in the UAE 33

the bride might be anywhere from twelve years upwards. Although Islam stipulates no special age for either the bride or groom, it is generally accepted that both must attain puberty. The average age at marriage of the older as well as the younger women interviewed was 16 or 17 years. The major complaint of the older women was the early age of marriage, for they felt unprepared for it and, in addition, it was at times a detriment to their physical health (specifically, problems related to pregnancy sometimes resulted). Nowadays, marriage is being postponed for most girls because of the educational opportunities available. The government has also supported a delay in marriage by passing mandatory education laws. Although families cannot be forced to keep their daughters in school, most families are aware of the benefits of a good education because they have traveled abroad and seen what it has meant for other women. Therefore, they want their daughters to be equally well educated. A natural outgrowth of this is that, whereas the groom was traditionally nearly twice the age, or more, of his bride, today's groom is closer to his bride in age.

In accordance with the rules of Islam and tribal traditions, the *mahr*, or bride-price, has always been paid directly to the bride. She usually purchases gold or silver, thus establishing for herself a form of economic security in case of a divorce or widowhood. The full amount is not usually paid at once, so that, if a man does consider divorce, he will think twice before finally making a decision because it may prove to be an economic hardship for him to provide the rest of the *mahr*.

Before oil wealth and the expanded employment opportunities that accompanied it, a man had to wait a long time before he could save sufficient funds to pay the bride's dowry and so marriage might occur late in life. Of course the *mahr* then was not very high but even saving a few extra *riyals* meant years of hard work and/or sacrificing. Setting aside savings for the bride-price nowadays, however, has become just as difficult a task. While it was recommended by the Prophet that the sum be at least ten *dinars*, no maximum is given, although it was assumed that it would be within reason and usually a token amount, as had traditionally been the practice. However, with the discovery of oil and the spread of wealth, *mahr* has skyrocketed and has nearly soared out of control, costing the prospective groom anwhere from 50,000 to one million *dirhams*. It is now expected that the *mahr* will include not only the fixed price paid to the bride, but also a sum for her father, money for gold, clothing and household furnishings, and sufficient funds for the wedding celebration, which may last anywhere from one day to two weeks. Marrying off one's daughter has become a sort of

34   *Marriage and Family Life in the UAE*

competition, with families vying to set the highest possible dowry for their daughters. As was related to the writer in many interviews, often the girl does not receive all the money because her father or male guardian may use it towards a business investment for his own personal gain.[14] This would never happen in the case of a girl from a wealthy family though, and her parents would be more concerned with the family she would marry into rather than the *mahr* alone, as maintaining prestige is their prime interest.

While the girls themselves regard marriage as the prime form of 'social security' as well as an important religious obligation, they place the blame for the high *mahrs* on the parents, and state that the ever-increasing sums make them feel like merchandise being auctioned off. As a religious obligation, they are aware of the merits of bride-price but insist that it should be a reasonable amount. They are aware that many of the men are marrying girls from outside the Emirates (many Indians and Egyptians, especially) and fear for their own marriage prospects if this trend continues.

The UAE government has even intervened to put an end to the high dowries by passing a law limiting the *mahr* to a maximum of 10,000 *dirhams*, but this has met with little success. Eventually, however, this practice will have to stop, and the key to scaling down the average *mahr* may well lie in the continued practice of local men marrying foreign women. As more men become unwilling to pay the high sums, parents will be forced to reconsider the effects this will have on their daughters' futures.

Transfer of the Bride: Family Life in the New Family Unit

Once married, the groom traditionally took the bride to live with him and his family. Only in rare cases did the groom move in with the bride's parents. In particular, if her family insisted that she was still too young to leave home, the groom was forced to live with her family for several years. In either case, the groom's inability to set up his own household, primarily for economic reasons, meant living with one or the other of the families until such time that he could afford his own home.

The trend toward individual homes is greater today, and it certainly is the ideal. That is not to say, however, that all ties are broken with either spouse's family once marriage takes place, because the bride remains dependent, throughout her life, on her family should any marital problems arise. It is important that she foster a good relationship with her in-laws, especially if she continues to live with them, but this tie is not as important as that between her and her own family. For this

Marriage and Family Life in the UAE 35

reason, many women are reluctant to marry if it means moving far from their families, or they may try to convince the men to settle in their (the women's) communities.[15]

Traditionally, once a woman produced her first male heir she held a higher position, and the mother-in-law, who holds the highest female position in any Arab family, would be less demanding. Especially in the instance when the son has married outside the family, and against his mother's wishes (as it is often that the mother pushes for maternal-cousin marriages), the mother-in-law/daughter-in-law relationship can be very fragile. This is a major reason why the bride would be hesitant to move far away from her family at the beginning of her marriage. Once the new bride's place in the family is firmly established, particularly after the time of the birth of the first child, good relationships will have been formed, and the bride is treated as one of the daughters might be. This continues to be the situation for brides today. There always was and will remain strong reverence for the parents, and the mother especially, but this does not have to stand in the way of a peaceful marriage. Whatever problems that might surface are, apparently, quickly and easily solved, as the majority of women interviewed indicated that they have very good relations with their in-laws.[16]

Within her new home, the UAE woman remains content to deal primarily with family responsibilities. During the period when the men left their homes for months at a time to engage in pearl-diving or other occupations in the Gulf region, the woman alone was responsible for the welfare and care of the family, and so her position as a decision maker in the family was very important. She continues to participate in the decision-making process as an equal partner to her husband[17] and 'family affairs' were noted as the primary topics of discussion between a husband and wife.

In addition, the writer found the husband-wife relationship to be very close. This is probably due to the fact that the husband and wife have more time together, and there is a chance to build a really firm relationship and share such common interests as poetry, literature, local politics and even business (listed as the favorite topics of conversation, after 'family matters', between husband and wife). Furthermore, in response to a question about whom they would turn to for advice if a personal problem arose, a large number of the younger wives said they would consult their husbands, while many of the older wives stated that they would seek the advice of the family elders or their parents. This also seems to indicate a closer husband-wife bond. An overwhelming majority of women who were asked whether they would give their

36 *Marriage and Family Life in the UAE*

husbands financial assistance if needed, assuming of course that the women had the resources, responded affirmatively. Even though Islamic law stipulates that the husband is responsible for all household needs, and that therefore the woman is allowed to spend her personal money in any way she chooses, there were no second thoughts about giving money to the husband. A willingness to assist the husband implies the existence of trust and confidence. Indeed, if a woman felt that her husband considered her to be 'degraded or inferior', as Wendell Phillips claims is the case,[18] it is unlikely that such positive responses would have been given. However, the respondents' emphatic positivism was sufficient evidence that these women do not have such self-images, nor is it likely, do their husbands. On the basis of the replies to these questions, as well as other supportive information gathered in interviews, close husband-wife relationships seem to be the rule rather than the exception.

In the settled areas, when most of the commodities needed by the family were produced at home, the bulk of the work was left to the women. They tended the livestock, carried the water from the wells to their homes in large water pots, collected the sticks for firewood, sewed, cooked, cleaned and reared the children. There was no one to help out unless there was another wife or an unmarried sister-in-law living with them. The Bedouin woman's life was even tougher as, in addition to all these chores, she had to weave and continuously put up the tent. She also wove the wool and made cheese which was sold to the sedentary people. The men's contribution to the running of the household was that they went to the market and made what few purchases were necessary, and, if an animal needed slaughtering, they did it.

Today, the upkeep of the house continues to be reserved for the women, although the men still make most of the important purchases. Many families have servants to do the household chores, so the women have been relieved of some of their domestic duties, and the availability of such modern appliances as stoves and refrigerators has eased their load a great deal, too.

Finally, women now have free time at their disposal, primarily when the children are at school in the morning, so they can cater to their own personal needs. Some attend literacy classes, or visit the local women's social center, while others visit friends and neighbors or shop for personal items. Men, too, have more available free time, and when women were asked how the men spend their day, the most common responses, after 'at work', were, with their friends, at home with their family, attending literacy classes, at sports clubs, the cinema, hunting or

Marriage and Family Life in the UAE 37

fishing. It is obvious that the extra-familial activities for both male and female have greatly increased in the past 10-15 years.

An important facet of marriage and family life in the UAE is the practice of female veiling and seclusion. Purdah, as it has been and continues to be practiced today, is beyond the rules as established by Islam. It is primarily because of the tribal tradition of honor being determined by the chastity of women that this tradition has lasted up to the present time.[19] In the Emirates, it was the parents and then the husband who decreed the wearing of the *burqu'* and *'abayah.* Once the girl reached puberty, usually around 13-14 years of age, she was completely secluded in the home and put on the *burqu'.* No one saw her except her parents, brothers and sisters, and those men who were her 'milk' brothers, and she remained in the house until the day she married.

The *burqu'* is an extra facial covering used in the Emirates, Qatar and Oman. It is removed only during prayers, and, since women pray at home, there is no fear of men seeing their faces. It was supposedly brought over from India centuries ago, and was adopted by both the settled and Bedouin women. The use of it, therefore, is in no way connected with an Islamic tradition, and there is no mention of its existence during the early Islamic period.

Although it is slowly disappearing among the settled communities, the *burqu'* continues to be used among the Bedu and newly settled populations. When the writer visited several of the new Bedouin settlements on the outskirts of Abu Dhabi, she observed that the *burqu'* worn there covered much more of the face than that used by women in the cities. Also, women in these settlements were more secluded, probably because the Bedouin are still not used to living in settled communities and close to town where their womenfolk are exposed to foreign men. This is a radical change from the isolation and security of the desert, where decades could pass and one might not see a foreigner.

Among the *Hadar*, or settled peoples, the *burqu'* began to disappear about 20-25 years ago, around the time schools began opening in Dubay and Sharjah. Slowly, as more and more schools opened in the 1960s and 1970s in Abu Dhabi, 'Ajman, Ras Al-Khaymah, and the smaller states, and as more people went abroad and became aware of other customs, fewer girls were forced to don the *burqu'.* Most would agree that the *burqu'* is on its way out and whether or not the *'abayah* will last is also a question now being asked by UAE women.[20] Already in Dubay and Sharjah, where the *burqu'* first began to disappear, more and more young women are not wearing the *'abayah*, especially those

38 *Marriage and Family Life in the UAE*

who have studied in Egypt, Kuwayt and abroad.

Not all of the resistance to unveiling comes from men. Many women are also greatly opposed to this 'invasion of their privacy'. There are instances when the husband insists the wife not wear the *burqu'* and it is the woman who stubbornly continues to wear it. This writer met many women (in Abu Dhabi, especially, as tribal traditions are still most closely observed there) who were urged by their families and friends to remove the *burqu'* but insisted on retaining it. When asked why they persisted in using it, most often the reply was that they were too 'shy' to go without it. The *burqu'* had become so natural a part of them that they could not speak freely without it, several said. Their predicament is very similar to that of Lebanese women forty years ago, who were also just beginning to unveil; as described by Muhammed Naccache:

> Just as it is inhuman to force a young girl to wear the veil today so it is also to make an old woman, who has been accustomed to wear the veil all her life, unveil in the name of progress.[21]

None of these women want their daughters to wear the *burqu'*, but taking off the *abayah* is another matter entirely. Perhaps the greatest fear expressed in interviews is that with the removal of the *'abayah* will come a lowering of moral standards. Many UAE men and women fear that removing the *'abayah* will automatically lead to a decadent form of social life.

When the writer asked for opinons on other Arab women, many UAE women responded that traditional Islam must not be sacrificed for progress, as has happened in some Arab states. It was obvious from their answers that these women are most intent on preserving religious customs and are determined to avoid the 'distasteful' cultural habits that Western-oriented development often brings. Their intentions are laudable and plausible. For this reason the *'abayah* may not be dropped soon, if at all. However, a look at the successes of their Gulf sisters in Kuwayt and Bahrayn should allay their fears that decadence is the only alternative to unveiling.

Veiling and seclusion have not necessarily meant the lack of family activities, and, although one might not find parents and children taking strolls together or eating in restaurants, as is done in the West, they do participate in other activities together. Before air-conditioning, many families spent the hot summer months camping at various oases. This pastime continues today, but for one or two days only instead of

Marriage and Family Life in the UAE   39

several months. Visiting relatives and friends in distant parts of the Emirates is also a family affair. Shopping, dining-out and attending the cinema are enjoyed in a group when abroad, but, in general, not at home, as they do not form part of the social customs.

The intermingling of men and women outside the immediate family rarely occurs. Among the few cases where intermingling of male and female does exist, this is between married couples only. In all cases, either the husband or the wife is not from the Emirates, and because in their own country mixed gatherings are permitted, they continue this practice while in the UAE. For example, if a local girl were married to a Kuwayti man she would more likely than not attend dinners with him at the homes of other 'mixed' couples. This would not happen, however, if both man and wife were from the Emirates. If a local or non-local man invites a local man to dinner, the wife would never accompany him. In the case of the women's dinners for their female friends, young children might also accompany the mother.

For the most part, the bulk of a woman's time is spent with other women, and, therefore, inter-female relationships are very important. Traditionally, the women with whom one grew up remained lifelong friends, and they all formed a 'group' because, once one attained puberty, there were no chances of going out and meeting new women. For this reason the majority of women interviewed had very close ties with the other women with whom they associated. All precautions are taken not to insult a 'group' member or to put oneself in a position to be ostracized. Previously, if this happened to a woman, the chances of her being able to join another 'group' were slim. Although several examples of women being excluded from a group were cited during interviews, such situations rarely occurred, mainly because women are so aware of the importance of friendship, and, therefore, are careful not to cause offense.

Increasingly, and especially among the younger women, it has become much easier to make new friends, and so it is not as necessary to cling to the same circle of women. By attending school, day or afternoon literacy classes, mothers' social centers, and women's organizations, for example, it is possible, and likely, that one will continue to meet new people. Thus, different kinds of friendship can be fostered separate from those shared with neighbors and relatives.

Children: Their Position in the Family

For most women, marriage is a form of stability or social security: and for Muslim women and men it is strongly recommended in the Qur'an.

40 *Marriage and Family Life in the UAE*

The importance of children to this bond cannot be underrated as their presence in many cases is what makes marriage a success, not only in the UAE but throughout the Muslim World. It is said that the Prophet himself stated that it is better to have a not-so-beautiful, fertile wife than a beautiful, unfertile wife, as proof of the significance of child-bearing in Islam. Barrenness is everywhere looked upon as a great shame, and no attempt to remedy this is left untried by Arab women.[22]

In the UAE, there is a preference for large, as opposed to small, families and most women over 25 stated that they would be happy with 'whatever number of children God gives'. While many younger women express a preference for 3-4 children, birth control is not widely practiced.[23] The government encourages large-size families in order to create the necessary labor pool that will allow the country to lessen its dependence on foreign workers in the future. Thus local families are offered financial incentives to have more children. Education and health care is provided free of charge to all citizens, and, in addition, every needy child is given a monthly stipend to pay for food, clothing and other expenses.

For most of the women interviewed, an 'ideal' life was described as either having a 'happy' family or a successful marriage; in both cases children are involved, for without children it is not likely that the marriage will last. If the wife is sterile, the possibility of the husband remarrying is high. Infertility is of course an acceptable reason for practicing polygamy in Islam. Some legal schools maintain that divorce is also acceptable if the husband is sterile, so there is no conflict with policy and practice here.

Understandably, women become a little nervous if they do not become pregnant right after marriage. However, because of the practice of child marriage, often their bodies have not fully developed by the time they do marry so it may not be until after several years of marriage that they begin reproducing.[24] For this reason, many of the older women are in favor of their daughters waiting a bit longer before marrying, so that they will not experience the same anxieties as their mothers.

Although most women express contentment with begetting either sons or daughters, the men definitely prefer boys because it is through boys that a man's social prestige is enhanced. Therefore, the wife feels that she has disappointed her husband if she does not produce male children.[25] Bearing male children is no guarantee that the husband will not remarry anyway, but with polygamy increasingly frowned upon, a man would be hard pressed for a good excuse if he did decide to remarry when his first wife had provided him with a male heir.

Marriage and Family Life in the UAE 41

On being asked to describe their personal ambitions, the majority of married women interviewed saw their family life as an extension of their own lives. Therefore, their personal sense of accomplishment was measured by how successfully they had served their families. Self-fulfillment was seen in terms of raising their children to be well-educated and socially productive UAE citizens.[26] With that in mind, it is not surprising that the bulk of a woman's lifetime is spent raising and caring for her children; even after they are grown and married.

There are no 'rules' as to the proper rearing of boys and girls although it is expected that after a certain age the boy will begin following his father, and will join the men in their own *majlis*. Up to that time, however, the mother is responsible for raising both sons and daughters. Should any problems or questions arise regarding their health or schooling, for example, she would, of course, turn to her husband for advice, as well as her own parents or the family elders (especially if the husband was not present, for some reason). The mother generally does devote more time to the child-rearing task than the father, which perhaps explains why the Prophet urged deep respect and honor for the mother.

Usually at the age of seven or eight, once he has acquired some knowledge of Islam, the boy begins attending mosque for prayers with his father. Although women do not attend the mosque, by the time girls are seven they have been taught the rudiments of Islam and begin praying at home with their mother. Up to that age, children are found playing together in the women's section. By the age of ten, however, more time is spent with one's own sex group, and the boys begin eating regularly with the men while the girls stay by their mother's side. The mother-son, brother-sister bonds remain tight forever though, regardless of the separation into different social worlds. And, during old age, although parents expect help from both their sons and daughters, most of the responsibility falls to the son, as the daughter's husband may not be in favor of assuming such a duty since he-may have his own parents to take care of. Also, should a sister become divorced or widowed after the death of the father, it is likely she would join her brother's household, so these close relationships are bound to be sustained throughout each's lifetime.

Thus, it is easy to see why such a high value is placed on children. For men, the more sons they have, the greater prestige they feel. For women, motherhood is seen as their prime goal in life for from this, it is hoped, will come a solid marriage.[27] Although modernization is bound to have an effect on their attitudes, and families may grow

42   *Marriage and Family Life in the UAE*

smaller as a result of later marriage and women's desire to work as well as be mothers, the motherhood role and the responsibilities it entails are not likely to change drastically in the near future.[28] In none of these practices is there conflict with Islam, nor is there likely to be as long as modernization is pursued with the traditional customs in mind.

Polygamy and its Effect on the Family

The practice of polygamy has been declining throughout the Muslim world. However, among the Arab states, only Tunisia has actually outlawed polygamy, although various other states have put mild restrictions on it.[29] In the UAE, to date, there are no laws restricting polygamy, so there is really only a man's conscience to stop him from practicing it. Polygamy definitely is becoming a thing of the past though, primarily because of women's influence.

Even though Islam allows a man up to four wives, polygamy was never very widely practiced in tribal society except by the ruling *shaykhs.*[30] Previously, a man might terminate an unsatisfactory union by divorce and then remarry, but trying to maintain two or more households was beyond the financial capacity of the average man.[31] Now, however, even when a man can afford more than one wife, the social, as well as familial, pressures are so great against polygamy that it is not widely practiced in the UAE, nor is it likely to be in the future. The reasons for this are many. For one, unless a man's wives are located in different towns, there is bound to be trouble between them. The mere possibility of family turmoil prompts most women to state that there are no advantages at all to polygamy. A few of those women who were part of such a household sanctioned it in cases where one wife was ill or sterile, or if the husband was equally fair to each wife, as demanded by Islam — but these were in a very small minority. On the whole, it is felt that polygamy causes instability in the family because the wives, as well as the children, are constantly in competition for the attention and love of the husband and father, which, legally, must be equally distributed. Nowadays, if faced with a husband who may remarry without just cause, a wife may insist on divorce beforehand, rather than be subjected to sharing a husband. Most importantly, the men as well as the women want to be considered 'modern' and, since monogamy is a trait of 'modern' societies, so they, too, must adopt this practice.[32] The last factor alone has had the greatest effect on restraining the practice of polygamy all through the Arab East.[33]

Marriage and Family Life in the UAE 43

Divorce and Widowhood

As previously stated, Bedouin women in general have traditionally held a relatively strong position in the marriage situation; thus, a woman in the UAE has it easier than most Arab women if she should decide to terminate a marriage. In general, it is more difficult for an Arab woman than an Arab man to secure a divorce, as a woman must present definite reasons for her decision whereas a man is not obliged to do so. However, divorce is by no means encouraged by Islam, so at any time that repudiation is practiced, the cause must be legitimate, or a wrong has been committed. Furthermore, the husband and wife are urged to seek advice and assistance in attempting to reconciliate before divorce is decided upon.

If a UAE woman decides life is unbearable with her spouse, she usually returns to the home of her parents, explains the situation to them, thus, hopefully, gaining their support, and the husband will feel forced either to try and win her back, or to give her the divorce so as to escape possible ridicule.[34] In some cases, the woman, without any outside assistance from her parents, succeeds in coaxing her husband to divorce her. In the case nowadays of a younger woman forced to marry a much older man, the woman may find the relationship unbearable because, for example, the husband is extremely conservative and may insist that she remain in the house at all times, rather than be allowed to continue schooling. She may keep complaining to him about her lack of freedom and desire to study until he becomes angry enough to divorce her, in which case he would be forced to pay whatever dowry had been held back at the time of the marriage.[35] Otherwise, if it is the woman who demands the divorce, she must pay back to her husband whatever bride-price she has received.

Divorce is increasingly frowned upon by the younger educated couples today, although no stigma is attached to a divorced woman and remarriage is not difficult. Incompatibility was cited as the prime circumstance under which divorce was justifiable, followed by the illness or infertility of either spouse. Now, however, since there is more effort made to give the girl a say in choosing her future husband, incompatibility, especially, is less of a problem and the divorce rate is decreasing.[36]

A divorced woman always returns to the home either of her parents or of a brother if the parents are deceased. Formerly, if she did not remarry, she was dependent solely on her family for economic support. Her dowry served as a sort of security, if she was able to keep it after the divorce, but her family paid for her food, clothing and other needs.

44   *Marriage and Family Life in the UAE*

Now, however, the government provides this service through the Ministry of Social Affairs, and every divorced woman is assured of an income if she needs it, thus becoming less of a financial burden to her family. And if she is given custody of the children, they, too, are provided for by the government although, legally, the husband is responsible for their upkeep. Where children are involved in divorce cases, whichever legal school one espouses, those are the rules followed in regards to guardianship, custody and support. In most cases, however, the son stays with the mother until age seven, and the daughter up to age nine. Then they are handed over to their father who, thereafter, is responsible for their rearing.

If marriage ends through widowhood, depending on the age of a woman and that of her children, she may or may not return to her family. An older woman with grown children would, of course, stay in her own home. If she had a son, he would then take on the responsibility of caring and providing for his mother unless she remarried, at which point the responsibility passed to the new husband. Otherwise, a widow too is now eligible for government assistance if she has no means of support.

Remarriage for both the divorced and the widowed woman has been traditionally easier for the Gulf woman than for other Arab women, mainly because no stigma is attached to her position. Remarriage is common, and indeed expected, especially if the woman is young, attractive, or from a good family. The dowry may be lower but this is not necessarily always the case. However, in all cases, if a woman marries a second time, her opinion is asked and the final decision is hers; thus a woman is forced to experience an arranged marriage only once in her life. For both the widowed and the divorced woman, the waiting period prescribed by Islam is observed before remarriage.

The Single Woman: A New Social Actor

In a society where marriages are arranged at an early age by the parents, it is very difficult even to locate a single woman. However, now that there is an alternative to early marriage, more girls are opting for an education before taking on the responsibilities of a house and children. And with bride-price continuing to soar, some girls who are ready to marry cannot because the men are not willing or are unable to meet the demands of the girls' families. It is possible now to meet women in their mid- and late twenties who are still unmarried, a phenomenon that would not have existed in this area fifteen to twenty years ago.

Previously, a girl was kept in seclusion until the time of marriage,

Marriage and Family Life in the UAE 45

and rarely went beyond the confines of her home after attaining puberty. She was confined to her room, as it were, and it remained improper for a young girl beyond puberty to sit in the company of married women because their conversation might include personal topics unsuitable for a young, unmarried girl to hear.

Once schools were built, families slowly became used to their daughters coming and going to classes, and, increasingly, the girls became less confined to their rooms. It is still not customary for young single women to sit with married women, but now there are other activities that young women can involve themselves in. Of those single women who never had a chance to go to school, many are returning to afternoon literacy classes. And for those young women who have completed their schooling, many take on jobs which keep them busy as well as provide a great social service.

The young women of 'Ajman, Umm Al-Qaywayn and Sharjah are particularly fortunate as clubs for them are being set up alongside the newly built women's societies. The idea behind forming the youth clubs was that, since the women's societies cater primarily to the married woman, there should also be a center for the young unmarried woman. Nursery schools for children are also being built. There are facilities for such activities as bowling, sewing, typing and swimming. A cinema and restaurant are being included so that girls have a place to entertain their friends, as eating in public places is not permitted, and attending the public cinema is not allowed by all parents. In Dubay and Sharjah, it is not unsual for groups of girls to go on day-trips to the villages of Kelba and Khor Fakkan without the accompaniment of elders, and it is acceptable for some of them to drive their own cars.

The generation of women in their twenties has experienced by far the most change, having been among the first to benefit from oil wealth. Not only do they want more than their parents had, but their parents have great aspirations for them, too. Of course, there will always be the odd case of a mother not wishing her daughter to leave the house for fear of what the outside world holds, but the great majority of mothers want their daughters to earn college degrees before they settle down to married life. By living out their youth, studying and traveling abroad, single women return with other views of what life should be, and, though they are intent on marrying a local man, their marriage life will not be completely traditional. Many want to open their own businesses or pursue careers as well as raise a family, and, as will be discussed later, daughters of some of the better-known families have already done so. About ten years ago it was primarily single women who were the van-

46 *Marriage and Family Life in the UAE*

guard of change when they were the first to take employment positions before it had become socially acceptable for women to work. And society has responded positively to their needs, through such organizations as youth clubs, and has responded positively to their demands, through government mandatory education laws, which indirectly delay marriage and provide official encouragement for women's career pursuits. It is likely that single women will continue to be the leaders of fundamental societal change as they forge ahead in their educational and professional pursuits. Later, when these women are married, the upbringing of their own families will reflect their new and transformed attitudes on life in general.

Conclusion

As Ruth Woodsmall noted in her follow-up study of Eastern Muslim women, many have conserved the rich values of the past and assimilated new values at the same time so as to meet the needs of the twentieth century.[37] In regard to marriage and family life in the UAE, the valued traditions of Islam and tribal society continue to be observed and respected, although room for change is also being provided. New educational opportunities have done most to raise women's status in the sphere of marriage and family life by ending child marriages. Marriage will continue to be the prime goal of the great majority of UAE women as it is seen as a form of social security, and in this respect marriage holds the same significance for most of the world's women. While the unsettled university woman looks forward to graduation as the most important time in her life, married women happily reminisce on the joys of their wedding day and their first experience with motherhood and note these as the most meaningful periods of their lives.

Fundamental changes in marriage and family life are taking root, beginning with equal educational and social advantages for women. Women are becoming recognized as independent personalities, for, as they assume roles outside the family and contribute to the building of their society, so their position within the family is elevated. An indication of this is that the terms of marriage are changing, and a daughter is less willing to accept whatever marital mate is chosen by her parents. No matter how simple divorce and remarriage may be according to Islamic or tribal custom, that is not what women want. Here the enlightened woman craves stability, and she will do her utmost to see that her marriage succeeds. This is one trait of modern societies she will gladly adopt. And the dozen or so men whom the writer also interviewed felt very strongly about this, too. Continual divorce or resort to

Marriage and Family Life in the UAE 47

polygamy are not longer the acceptable solutions to incompatible marriages. Rather than treating the cure (i.e., constant remarriage), treating the illness is what is desired, and this can be done within a traditional framework and without defying the rules of Islam. By allowing women more flexibility in their roles as daughters and sisters, as increasingly occurs today, an improvement in their status and functions as wives and mothers is inevitable, and incompatibility in the marriage and problems in the family unit will occur less frequently.

Notes

1. 'Putting Their House in Order', *The Middle East*, no. 48 (October 1978), p. 74.
2. Muhammad Abu Zahra, 'Family Law' in Majid Khadduri and Herbert Liebesny (eds), *Law In the Middle East*, vol. 1 (Middle East Institute, Washington, DC, 1955), pp. 132-3.
3. Mernissi, *Beyond the Veil*, pp. 18-20.
4. Noel Coulson, *Conflicts and Tensions in Islamic Jurisprudence* (Chicago University Press, Chicago, 1969), p. 25.
5. All children nursed by the same woman, whether or not they are blood-related, are, thereafter, considered brothers and sisters and can never intermarry.
6. Majid Khadduri, 'Marriage in Islamic Law: The Modernist View-points' in *The American Journal of Comparative Law*, vol. XXVI (Spring 1978), p. 217.
7. Abu Zahra, 'Family Law', pp. 138-40.
8. Ibid., pp. 141-4.
9. Ibid., pp. 148-50.
10. Ibid., pp. 151-8. Also, see Subhi Mahmasani, 'Transactions in the Shari'a' in Khadduri and Liebesny (eds), *Law In The Middle East*, vol. 1, pp. 196-8.
11. Those few women who had chosen their own spouses were primarily young girls, between the ages of 20-25, from Dubay and Sharjah, who had studied in Kuwayt and met their husbands at the University. (Local women may also marry Saudis, Omanis, or other Gulf men, but marriages to men outside the Gulf region are unheard of.)
12. Lienhardt, 'Social Aspects of Trucial States', p. 226.
13. Jeffery, 'The Family in Islam', p. 46.
14. This problem is not unique to the UAE or to the Arab world. See, for example, 'Who Will Buy My Sweet Ripe Daughter?' *The Middle East* (August 1978), pp. 58-9.
15. Lienhardt, 'Social Aspects of Trucial States', also made this observation, pp. 225-6.
16. William Goode, 'Changing Family Patterns', pp. 139, 142-3 discusses other possible bases for mother-in-law/daughter-in-law problems.
17. The vast majority of the women interviewed confirmed and even stressed this point.
18. Wendell Phillips, *Unknown Oman*, p. 145.
19. Refer to pages 18-19 of this study.
20. 'Aba' aw la 'Aba'? '*Sawt Al-Umma*' (Sharjah) (May 22, 1978), p. 8.
21. Muhammed Naccache as quoted in Peter Mansfield, *The Arabs* (Penguin, London, 1977), p. 540.

48 Marriage and Family Life in the UAE

22. Goode, 'Changing Family Patterns', p. 112.

23. Whether or not birth control is permitted by Islam is questionable. Some scholars say that it is not, on the basis of Sura XVII:31, while others claim it is. For further discussion, see Abdul-Rauf, *Islamic View of Women and the Family*, pp. 124-5.

24. This was the comment of several women's doctors interviewed by this researcher.

25. Refer back to section on tribal traditions in Ch. 1, p. 19. Also Gabriel Baer, *Population and Society*, p. 37.

26. This is not unusual for women, in general, because, as defined by Viola Klein, *The Feminine Character – History of an Ideology*, p. 9, if one adopts the Muller-Lyer classification of the historic development of society into three main phases – the Clan Epoch, the Family Epoch and the Individual Epoch – according to the social unit which ideologically forms the basic element of the social organization at a given time period, it is not until a society adopts a capitalist-type economy that there is a shift from the family phase to the individual phase. At that point, women, for example, begin thinking more in terms of themselves as individuals, with their own goals and perspectives separate from those of their family. That is not to say that this will definitely occur among UAE women, but if one looks at the studies of Egyptian women, as described by Morroe Berger, *The Arab World*, pp. 127-32, over the years there has been a move toward smaller families, insistence on maintaining careers after marriage, and a preference for later marriage so schooling can be completed – all signs of a desire for increased emancipation and more personal freedoms than their mothers or grandmothers would ever have considered.

27. A note of possible interest is that the vast majority of women interviewed said they were only addressed as 'umm – ' in the presence of visitors; otherwise their husbands always called them by their first names.

28. An example of this is that in interviews with female university students, their concept of ideal family size was very close to that of less educated, younger (up to age 25) married women – 3-4 children.

29. N. Anderson, *Law Reform*, pp. 110-14.

30. Refer back to page 19 of this study.

31. Dearden, *Arab Women*, p. 13. 'Unsatisfactory' usually meant that the wife was infertile.

32. Ibid., p. 13.

33. El-Daghestani, 'Evolution of the Muslim Family', p. 349.

34. Lienhardt, 'Social Aspects of Trucial States', pp. 223-4.

35. Several such cases were related to this researcher by the women involved.

36. Among all of the divorced women the present researcher met, all were previously married to men they had never met or spoken with until the wedding night.

37. Ruth Woodsmall, *Women and the New East* (Middle East Institute, Washington, DC, 1960), p. 381.

3 THE ROLE OF EDUCATION IN RAISING THE STATUS OF THE UAE WOMAN

Islam and Education

There are many explanations as to why women were finally denied the right to be equally educated but basically the conclusion reached is that men feared for the honor of their womenfolk if they were allowed outside of the house. Although it was incumbent upon every Muslim to learn to read the Qur'an, there is little in the Scriptures relating to education or learning. Furthermore, there is nothing in the Qur'an, or in the *Hadith*, which reserves to males, exclusively, the right to learn. There is a saying that the Prophet urged his followers to pursue learning even as far away as China. But, again, this was not limited to men.

In the early Islamic period literacy meant being able to read the Qur'an. There was not much emphasis put on writing, however, as this was a skill needed by scribes, in particular, and not all that necessary for the common person.[1] There have been famous female Islamic scholars, poets and saints.[2] Since there is no organized priesthood in Islam, this should have made it easier for women to become saints, although most are mainly found among the Sufi orders. Many women also gained distinction as eminent scholars, especially for their knowledge of the *Hadith*. Slowly, however, women were pushed out of the limelight and forced to assume subordinate positions to men in their pursuit of acquiring and spreading knowledge.

With the intrusion of various local customs into Islam, women became less and less a part of social life in general. Once they attained puberty women were rarely let out of their homes for any reason, not even for the purpose of praying, let alone to obtain an education. Unless a woman had a father or older brother who felt girls should be encouraged to learn more and took it upon himself to teach her poetry and the *Hadith*, or another literary form, a woman never progressed beyond a grasp of the rudiments of Islam and the Qur'an. In defense of excluding women from mosques and public places, religious men cited Sura XXXIII:59 in which the Prophet's wives and followers were urged to cover up for fear of harassment. In addition, most fathers argued that, since women's only purpose in life was to marry, formal education would be wasted on girls. Finally, and perhaps most significantly, many men were afraid of the power that educated women might wield

50   The Role of Education

and feared some might feel encouraged to enter into illicit affairs. So the solution was segregation and seclusion of women and the denial of their right to an education.

As long as a person remains ignorant of her rights, no questions or problems arise. Thus, Muslim women remained passive and silent until the nineteenth century when missionary schools were introduced throughout various parts of the Middle East and thus educational reforms for women had to be made. Had it not been for the efforts of such men as Qasim Amin, who insisted that Islam was not against the education of women and who was among the first Muslim men to realize the value of an education to a woman as well as to her family, the process might have taken even longer. Perhaps not all men are convinced of the need to educate women, or even the right of women to an education, but the need to modernize has forced them to put many of these doubts aside momentarily, at least. However, this issue could resurface, especially in the various Arab countries where the once traditional male strongholds, such as white-collar jobs, might become temporarily open to women. Later, there might be an over-abundance of qualified workers in white-collar jobs, with males and females competing for the same jobs. Eventually, more men might be forced to look into ordinary industrial and agricultural positions if they were less qualified than the females − an alternative they would not quietly accept.[3] Should this occur, Muslim women would be better prepared to defend themselves because many are educated and aware of their rights as defined by Islam.

Education in the UAE

The relationship of the British with the shaykhdoms was unlike that which they shared with any other of their dependencies. Aside from maintaining free access to the trade routes, it was never the goal of the British to establish a formal colonial base in the area. Thus, during their domination of the region no significant changes in social or economic conditions were made. Up to the early 1950s and before the formation of the UAE, only the traditional *kuttabs* existed, where rote memorization of the Qur'an along with basic arithmetic was taught. Boys and girls attended the *kuttab*, sometimes together if there was only one instructor, with the boys sitting separately from the girls. At the age of ten, the girls were forced to leave school by their parents as, by this time, most were reaching puberty and would have to go into seclusion.[4]

When the first formal school was opened in Sharjah in 1953,

The Role of Education

teachers were provided by the Kuwayt Education Department. Kuwayt later opened schools in Dubay, Fujayrah, 'Ajman and Umm Al-Qaywayn which came under the administration of the Kuwayt Office opened in Dubay in 1963. Qatar also built eight schools in the northern Emirates and Saudi Arabia provided Ras Al-Khaymah with a religious institute as well as teachers. Bahrayn also provided a small number of teachers and the United Arab Republic sent an educational mission to Sharjah in 1958 which provided teachers for Dubay, Ras Al-Khaymah and Sharjah.[5]

Kuwayt provided by far the greatest amount of educational assistance and by 1971 there were 17,754 students enrolled in its schools – a great jump from the 230 pupils first enrolled in 1953.[6] The salaries of more than 700 teachers, as well as allowances, transportation, books, food, and construction and maintenance of 45 schools in the northern Emirates were all financed by Kuwayt. Other Arab countries provided and funded 200 other teachers but they were supervised by Kuwayt (Egypt – 65, Qatar – 57, Saudi Arabia – 34, Abu Dhabi – 12, Bahrayn – 9, and local teachers – 23).[7]

Technical schools were built by Britain in three of the states – Sharjah (1958), Dubay (1964) and Ras Al-Khaymah (1969) – and courses in carpentry, vehicle maintenance, electrical installation and mechanical engineering were offered. By 1971, there were 330 students enrolled in these three schools. In addition, teacher-training classes were set up at the secondary schools. One program was established for girls in Sharjah, and one for boys in Dubay, and a total of 159 students were enrolled in these two classes by 1971.[8] An agricultural school was opened up in Ras Al-Khaymah in the late 1950s – this, along with the technical schools, was Britain's main contribution to education in the shaykhdoms.[9]

When the United Arab Emirates was formed in 1971, educational needs were given top priority and the newly formed government's goal was to provide every child, female and male, with the best education available. The Kuwayti-administered schools were then turned over to the federal Ministry of Education when the union was formed. Now that the government had its own source of revenues, through petroleum discoveries, every child was assured access to educational institutions. Since 1971, the Ministry of Education's budget has increased fourteen-fold.[10] There are now 350 schools, in addition to the new UAE university, with a total enrollment of 94,425 students and 7,849 teachers.[11] To respond to the needs of the growing expatriate sector, a large number of private schools have also opened throughout the UAE.

52 The Role of Education

Although during the first two years of public education there were no facilities for female students, by 1955 girls were enrolling in the first school built for them in Sharjah. Initially, it was not unusual for a boy's family to permit him to board at the school if it was too far from home (especially for secondary education as only Dubay and Sharjah offered secondary level up to the 1960s). However, the idea of girls boarding was not popular, and if an area had no facilities beyond intermediate level, that was where the girls' education ended. For this reason, until facilities for all levels were built in each shaykhdom, female enrollment was far behind that of the males.[12] It is not unusual for formal education to be available to boys earlier than to girls; similar attitudes are common in many developed countries today. And although universal coeducation is a rather distant prospect – if it comes at all – equal education for males and females does now exist.[13]

Both public opinion and official government policy favor the education of girls. There is little opposition to girls' education from parents, and there has been great success in the campaigns of individual rulers as well as of the education authorities in encouraging parents to keep their daughters in school.[14] Since the days of Kuwayti educational administration, incentives were provided in the form of a monthly stipend for each child, free meals, clothing, transportation, medical care and free school supplies.[15] All of these continue to be offered today, except for the monthly stipend which, since 1977, is now given to financially needy children only. Now, however, there really is a decreasing need for incentives as the families have become well aware of the benefits of an education for each of their children. The enthusiasm towards school is expressed by old and young; all are excited about the new opportunities to enrich themselves and their children and, as long as opportunities for both sexes are available, there is no need to favor son over daughter.

The ruling families have staunchly supported the education of females. Indeed, the example they set by sending their own daughters to school served as an incentive for other families to do the same. In the case of Abu Dhabi, especially, where setting up a formal school system meant literally starting from scratch because there were no educational institutions except for the *kuttabs* up to the mid-1960s, the support of Shaykh Zayid and his wife, Shaykha Fatima, has been most effective in encouraging local families to enroll their daughters in school. Shaykha Fatima, who is also pursuing her studies, personally visits many girls' schools in various parts of the UAE throughout the year and urges the girls to work hard and complete their schooling.[16]

The Role of Education

And if a student is facing difficulties at home – if, for example, her parents are not allowing her to continue with school – a request from the ruling family may help in changing their minds.[17] It might be added that the ruling families make frequent reference to the Prophet's love for learning as support for their argument that girls should be allowed to continue in school.

In the cities, it is no longer common for parents to refuse to send their daughters to schools. However, each school is assigned at least one social worker by the Ministry of Education to deal with female school drop-outs.[18] In recent years the number of girls leaving school early has declined, and when a student does drop out of school, every effort is made to bring her back. Termination of school as a result of marriage is the most common reason for girls leaving school[19] and this is related to the practice of arranging marriages when girls are very young. In most of these cases, the girl comes from a poor family, so the parents will benefit from her early marriage. Regardless of the mandatory education laws, the government cannot force parents to keep their daughters in school or delay marriage but in such cases the social worker attempts to persuade the family to keep the girl enrolled as long as possible. After the marriage the social worker visits the student in her home and speaks to her husband about permitting his wife to complete her education through the adult literacy program. In the great majority of cases, husbands agree.

Among the other problems education authorities face is the occasional mother who does not want her daughter attending classes because she is needed at home to help with the housework. There are also instances in which the girl is an only child and the parents do not want her to be away from them. Sometimes, girls who entered school at a late age choose to drop out because they are embarrassed by the fact that they are older than their peers. In several instances, a student had been harshly reprimanded by a teacher and felt too humiliated to return to school and face her friends.[20] In more than 15 schools visited by the writer, however, the number of students that had left school over the preceding two years was small. This relatively low drop-out rate indicates that the desire for learning is indeed widespread throughout the UAE, and any initial problems there may have been in enrolling girls in schools have now, for the most part, been overcome.

Efforts to instill parental interest in their children's education are made by the individual headmistresses through the formation of parent-teacher associations.[21] As many mothers are still not accustomed to being actively involved in their children's school lives, rates of partici-

54 *The Role of Education*

pation are sometimes low. Another reason for the limited success of these efforts is that the girls themselves do not tell their mothers about such events for fear that the instructors will use this opportunity to report on the girls' conduct or progress in school. Thus, attendance at most of these events is made up of parents of the expatriate students who have had prior experience with education-related meetings in their own countries. Through mother-daughter-teacher teas, holiday parties and various student projects interest has been increasing and local women's societies have also encouraged mothers to take an active part in their children's school activities.[22]

The structure of education is the same for both male and female.[23] The required courses for each are also the same — religion, history, math, science, Arabic and English and fine arts. Schedules differ only in the choice of electives: boys take wood-working and other manual-training courses while the girls take home economics (i.e., nutrition, hygiene, childhood development, sewing and cooking). Many sociologists are against schedule differentiation because it is felt this leads to the rigid defining of sex roles; i.e., so long as girls continue to study home economics only and not shop, too, they will always see themselves in the narrowly defined roles of wives and mothers. Developing countries, especially, are warned against adopting such programs from the start, in order that girls will pursue not only traditional fields but will enter areas which they are as equally qualified as men to fill, and in which they are badly needed.[24] The UAE might well take cognizance of this warning as there was a preponderance of males majoring in the sciences at the secondary level over the past five years while girls tended to favor the arts over the sciences.[25]

As previously stated, schools in the cities are segregated, right from the first grade. Only male teachers are assigned to teach boys, while female teachers are assigned to girls. However, in 1978, the Ministry of Education began experimenting with female teachers in some of the boys' primary schools.[26] In the small towns and Bedouin settlements, however, schools have been co-ed since they were first built in 1968. Because there are not enough students to warrant the building of two separate schools, boys and girls continue to attend school together. Since most of the schools are run by married couples, it is not unusual for girls to have male instructors part of the time. The parents do not object to this, for the most part, until girls reach the age of nine or ten.

As girls reach puberty, problems arise. At that point many parents begin pulling their daughters out of school unless arrangements for segregated classes are made. Sometimes the problem is solved by

The Role of Education 55

sending the male students to board at schools in the cities but then there is the problem of teachers. Unless qualified female instructors can be persuaded to teach in these areas, girls cannot attend because their parents no longer want them taught by male instructors.

A coeducational system is not feasible in the UAE because of local customs relating to veiling and seclusion, and no amount of persuasion or reference to Islam's encouragement of education for females will change the attitudes of the parents. This problem must therefore be reckoned with if the drop-out rate for girls in the villages is to be lowered and if females in these areas are to be given a fair chance at a complete formal education.[27]

Vocational Education Programs for Females

There are also several vocational education centers in the UAE which serve as alternatives to the traditional education system. Those available for females are the teacher-training institute in Sharjah and the nursing school in Abu Dhabi. The enrollment of local girls in both of these institutions is not very high, considering that teaching and nursing are the two most acceptable professions for women in a segregated society. Enrollment in the teaching institute reached a peak of 121 students in 1974 but has been dropping ever since.[28] This is explained by the fact that more girls would prefer to pursue a university degree, rather than simply obtain a teaching certificate, which is only equivalent to a secondary school diploma. With regard to nursing, there is also less incentive to enter the field because it is a rigorous career demanding long hours and hard work and, unfortunately, it is not highly respected in the Arab world.[29]

Acceptance into both the teaching and nursing programs is automatic for local women in order to encourage them to enter these fields. Upon completion of the preparatory level (grade 9), a girl may enroll in the four-year teaching program at the institute in Sharjah as an alternative to the traditional secondary school program. Any local woman who has completed grade 6 may register at Abu Dhabi's nursing school.[30]

Transportation is a problem and, since boarding is not an option, students who enter these schools are from the immediate area; i.e., the teaching institute is attended mainly by girls from Sharjah, and the nursing school is similarly attended by local girls. For this reason, Sharjah has a large reserve of teachers – several hundred – in its school system. In comparison, Abu Dhabi has only 4 or 5 local teachers. On the other hand, since the northern Emirates have no nursing school,

56　*The Role of Education*

there are no registered nurses in that area. Up to the present time, any woman who has been willing to become a nurse's aide has had to take on-the-job training – the only schooling available.[31] Since its opening in 1972, the nursing school in Abu Dhabi has been attended by only a handful of local Abu Dhabians and a number of students from other Arab countries who have settled in the area.[32]

Although Sharjah's teaching institute is for females only, the nursing school, which has programs for nurse's aides as well as nurses, is co-educational, and the school's policy has caused some families discomfort. Many parents are unwilling to permit their daughters to attend the nursing school for this reason. Since these females will eventually have to work with males anyway, there should not be such an objection, but many parents use this as an excuse to bar their daughters from attending. Generous stipends are given to all students and active campaigning has been conducted throughout the UAE to increase the enrollment, but to little avail. Since 1972, an average of six students per year have completed the three-year registered nurse's program and only one of these was a local woman.[33] Of the slightly higher number of nurse's aides who have graduated from the nursing school's one-year program, only five were local people. There are now plans for separate male and female facilities in the hope that more local women will be allowed to pursue nursing careers. It is also hoped that this will lead to a lessened dependence on foreign medical staff in the future. Nursing seems to be the best alternative for those girls who want to become doctors, but cannot get permission to study abroad by their parents. However, until more respect is accorded the career, it is not likely that many will take this option.

Higher Education – Women's Access to It

If a girl passes through preparatory level, it is probable that she will finish the secondary level also. At the secondary level there are less female than male drop-outs.[34] And, as the number of female high school graduates begins to swell, so does the number of female college aspirants increase.[35] Throughout the Gulf area, the desire for higher education for females has not been easily fulfilled, primarily because of local traditions forbidding an unmarried female to leave the house for any reason other than marriage. However, the pressure for modernization has proved stronger than tradition, and there has been an increasing number of college-bound Gulf women during the past decade. In Kuwayt, the problem was partially solved by building a university in the country, but its partly coeducational campus has made some

The Role of Education

parents hesitant about sending their daughters.[36] Saudi Arabia came closest to finding a solution by building a separate campus for its female students.[37] The UAE very wisely followed suit by opening its own university in 1977, with separate facilities for men and women.

Although many have criticized the establishment of a local university on the grounds that the society is not yet ready for such an institution,[38] Shaykh Zayid's dream of founding a university has proved the best way to prepare the society for higher education. It was necessary to open the university as soon as possible because the area needs a center of higher education to accustom local people to having access to all levels of education and to give opportunities to those who cannot leave the country. Therefore, the high costs associated with opening the university at Al-'Ain in November 1977, one year later than planned, were justified. The institution is not yet completely organized, and this may not happen during the first few years, as was the case with Kuwayt University. However, the more conservative families are now much less hesitant to allow their daughters to continue their education. And because of Shaykh Zayid's sponsorship, the university has become a symbol of UAE pride and progress.

Approximately 185 female students entered as part of the university's first enrollees in November 1977. Of the four faculties that were then set up – Education, Arts, Business Administration and Science – most females enrolled in the Education Department. During the next two academic years, faculties of Medicine, Islamic Studies, Agriculture, Law, and Regional Gulf Issues will also be added.[39] The number of males who entered in 1977 was only slightly greater than the number of females (approximately 300). Because more men are likely to continue their studies abroad, it is expected that the number of women at the university may soon exceed that of men. Having a local university has made higher education more accessible not only to single women but also to married women. A number of married women entered as part of the class of 1981, some residing alone in the university quarters and others with their husbands in special facilities for married students.

Free, government-sponsored higher education has been the right of every UAE citizen since the union was formed, and even before this Abu Dhabi gave generous scholarships to any shaykhdom national accepted for admission in a university abroad.[40] The daughters of the more liberal families, who have attended foreign universities for the past 15 years, will therefore continue to do so. Their numbers have increased year after year, but most continue to major in the social sciences and arts, with only a few pursuing engineering, medicine,

58 The Role of Education

business or law. Even if they do earn these more specialized degrees, their families may not permit them to accept work other than in the traditional field of education.[41] Moreover, because of the desire to keep local traditions intact, most families prefer to send their daughters to school close by. So Kuwayt University has long been the favorite choice for most UAE parents. The countries with the largest numbers of female enrollees in order of importance are Kuwayt, Egypt, Iraq and Lebanon. During the past few years, an ever-growing number of students have gone to Britain and the United States. In fact, admissions for males and females to American schools have more than doubled since 1975.[42]

Admittedly, there is a great deal of pressure on those female students studying abroad, for the example they set will determine whether many more girls will be permitted to follow in their footsteps. For those young women who study in the West, especially, the responsibility is even heavier because they have to deal with two very different cultures. On returning home they must be able to combine what they have learned in the West with the noble values and richness of their own culture. Undoubtedly, they will be able to meet this challenge, as have other women throughout the Arabian Gulf.[43]

The government is pushing strongly for female participation in all areas, and barriers to women's participation in all professions are starting to break down. Family pressures forced the first UAE female law graduate to accept a teaching position rather than a law-related one. However, the first female UAE petroleum engineer is now with the Abu Dhabi National Oil Company and a political science graduate is the first UAE female to be employed at the Ministry of Foreign Affairs. Employment positions for female graduates will continue to grow in number and variety through continued government support and increased family awareness as to the right and need of their daughters to be educated and their obligation, once their education is completed, to apply their knowledge to help build society.

Adult Education-Literacy Programs for Women

As part of the government's policy to provide educational opportunities for every citizen, regardless of sex or age, an adult education program has also been set up. The general enthusiasm for learning is perhaps nowhere better reflected than in the participants in this program. For the woman who has never had the opportunity to attend a formal school or who was not able to complete her schooling because of an early marriage, the evening program is a means to attain literacy or

The Role of Education

finish a degree. The success of the female adult literacy program is attributable to women's desire to prove to themselves and their male relatives that they are equally capable of learning and even of acquiring a degree.[44]

Enrollment in these classes is almost evenly divided between married and single women. The married woman's incentive comes from the first-hand knowledge that an uneducated wife impedes the family's progress as she is responsible for running the home and raising the children. The motto has been unconsciously adopted that when you educate a female you are educating her as well as her children. Knowing domestic arts, alone, is no longer sufficient for a woman, and women themselves admit that education is an important consideration when choosing a spouse to-day — men prefer educated wives and women prefer educated husbands.[45] Some women fear that their husbands may marry a second time because they are not adequately educated. This is not, of course, the only or primary reason for women's attendance at literacy classes. Whether married or single, the most important reason for enrolling is the traditional respect for learning. A learned woman gains not only self-respect but also 'respect and appreciation' from men.[46]

Many of the single women who enroll hope that their degree will lead to a promising job in a few years and some hope that their parents will allow them to continue with their schooling through university level if they work earnestly and complete their high school diploma.[47] Very few of the married women have this objective in mind when enrolling; the majority of them do not work now, nor do they plan to work in the future.

The adult literacy program is such that within two years one completes the equivalent of four years of primary education; thereafter the regular pace is followed and one can go on attending until the completion of secondary level. For many women who quit school to marry, or because their parents withdrew them at puberty, and who have but a few years left of studying in order to graduate, this is an ideal program. Otherwise, it is unlikely that a woman, especially if she has children, can afford to spend more than three or four years studying. Therefore, many women will leave after becoming literate rather than completing the program.[48] About 50 percent of those who finish primary level in the evening go on to the secondary stage. The women always come prepared for their classes and absenteeism is low.[49]

A very active campaign was initiated by the Ministry of Education to encourage men and women to attend classes. Here, again Shaykh Zayid and Shaykha Fatima have exerted strong influence to embolden

60   *The Role of Education*

women, especially, to enroll, and television and radio programs extolling the benefits of an education from religious and social perspectives were initially broadcast. Shaykha Fatima continues to visit the schools in the area throughout the year, and often checks with directresses to see that all is running smoothly and to offer any necessary assistance.

Until 1976, an allowance was given each person who enrolled; 200 dirhams for first-year students, 300 dirhams for second-year students, and so on. Transportation, books, stationery and other educational needs are still supplied free of charge and, at the end of the year, graduation parties are held at all schools and prizes are awarded to top students. Even without these incentives, though, the notion that an education reaps many benefits has definitely taken root in the UAE and the enthusiasm with which women, young and old, attend classes is unlike that witnessed in any developed country. Their thirst for knowledge seems almost insatiable as they progress from level to level. Beyond the traditional forms of education available, one ambitious group of women in Abu Dhabi, all of whom have at least secondary school degrees, has surged even further ahead, by forming its own foreign language program. Led by Shaykha Moza bint Hilal, they have established the program in order to benefit from their free mornings while their children are at school. In collaboration with the Ministry of Education's foreign language program for its own employees, these women have set up a schedule whereby they can also take French and English language courses during the times when government employees are not scheduled for classes. Over forty local women are now participating in this program, most of them studying both English and French at the same time, six days a week.

The desire for increased knowledge about other people's ways of life, as well as that of their own, has obviously always existed. Had it not been for the discovery of petroleum, women's aspirations might not have been realized because of the lack of resources. Now the door to knowledge is open wide and so it is likely to stay. Modernization and education go hand in hand and, for a nation in a hurry to catch up with its neighbors, an indication of wise and prudent planning is the early establishment of an educational system that will reach every member of society in remote as well as urban areas. This has been and continues to be the policy of the UAE government.

Conclusion

Unlike the kind of opposition King Faysal faced when opening a girls'

The Role of Education   61

school in 1960,[50] female education in the Emirates was almost universally welcomed. Perhaps the introduction of education for girls was facilitated by the fact that Kuwayt, Saudi Arabia, Bahrayn and Qatar were supporting such a policy in their own countries. If these very traditional Islamic states had been able to convince their citizens that education was a right to be enjoyed by all, according to Islam, then it was equally possible for the UAE to do so. Through constant quoting from the Qur'an and *Hadith*, Shaykh Zayid, as President of the union and ruler of the wealthiest state, encouraged the rapid spread of education and generously provided funds for any student willing and able to study abroad. He and Shaykha Fatima have continued to encourage the education of girls and have provided every opportunity to make this possible. One highly significant result of their efforts was the building of a local university so that parents would no longer have an excuse for not allowing their daughters to pursue higher education. Women here have not had to struggle for equal rights to education as they have in many other Muslim Arab states; it was handed to them on a silver platter. The issue of woman's rights in general is by no means an 'insignificant' one,[51] as members of ruling families and officials throughout the area have taken women into consideration in all development plans since the beginning of oil wealth and the ability to make such plans. It is a fervent hope, as well as an expectation, that educated women will apply their knowledge to the building up of UAE society. The desire by one and all to be part of a modern twentieth-century state has forced many restrictive tribal traditions to be put aside.

In every society, there no doubt exists a minority of men and women who would prefer that females remain second-class citizens and one way to accomplish this is by denying them access to various types and levels of education. Very little can be done about these individual cases except to hope that time will bring a change in attitude. In the UAE, men's general response to education for women is that it is a fantastic opportunity for them to enrich themselves, and, if one observes the arrivals of female evening program students, one sees that a good number of these come accompanied by their husbands. The combination of personal initiative and government sponsorship has been a successful one. Government spending on education has gone from 62.5 million dirhams in 1972, to 888 million dirhams in 1977, representing 8.6 percent of the federal government's budget. This covers all public schools through secondary level, as well as all technical and vocational schools, scholarships for university level students and

62 The Role of Education

generous subsidies to private schools also located in the UAE.[52]

As increasing numbers of educated women speak out and display to other women their courage in participating in the nation-building process, more women will undoubtedly come forward and use their acquired knowledge and skills, also. There is no fear of violating Islamic tenets as neither learning nor working is denied by Islam. As long as schools remain segregated, there should be no conflict with traditions which emphasize the honor of the womenfolk. Furthermore, as attending school becomes a *sunna*, or tradition, the Bedouins, too, may become staunch supporters of education.[53]

Notes

1. Fernea and Bezirgan, *Muslim Women Speak*, p. xxviii.
2. Abbott, 'Women', pp. 201-3, and Fernea and Bezirgan, *Muslim Women Speak*, pp. xxvii-xxix.
3. Boserup, *Women's Role in Economic Development*, pp. 133-4.
4. Several sources say the girls were not allowed to attend school at all, but the women themselves told the present writer that they did attend, but only up to age ten.
5. Hawley, *The Trucial States*, pp. 234-5.
6. Robert A. Mertz, *Education and Manpower in the Arabian Gulf* (American Friends of the Middle East Gulf Study, Washington, DC, 1972), pp. 150-1.
7. Ibid., p. 151.
8. Ibid., pp. 152-6.
9. Hawley, *The Trucial States*, pp. 236-7.
10. See Tables 1 and 2 in Appendix B.
11. 'Arab Education Ministers' Meet Opens Today', *Emirates News* (Abu Dhabi, April 18, 1978), p. 1.
12. See Table 1 in Appendix B.
13. It might also be noted that schools are still segregated in some European countries; see Alva Myrdal, 'Women Around the World — An Afterword', *The Center Magazine* (May-June 1974), p. 79.
14. Up-to-date literacy rates for nationals only are not yet available but there definitely has been a change since 1968 when, according to UN sources, 27 percent of the males and 8.9 percent of the females aged 15 and over were literate and 34.5 percent of the males and 16.2 percent of the females aged 15-20 were literate. *UN Demographic Year Book, 1971* (UN Pub., New York, 1971), Table 18. By 1975, these figures had increased to 44.7 per cent of the females and 60.4 per cent of the males aged 10 and over as being literate, according to the UAE Ministry of Planning's *Annual Statistical Abstract* (1977), p. 44. However, since nearly one-half of the UAE population belongs to the expatriate community it was not possible to determine from these available figures exactly what percentage represents UAE nationals and what percentage represents the expatriates.
15. This policy has been pursued in a number of Arab states. See Pierre Vernier, 'Education for Arab Girls, Economic Expansion, Changing Attitudes Favour Progress', *UNESCO Features*, no. 437 (April 1964), p. 15.
16. See, for example, 'Fatima's Call to Girl Students', *Emirates News* (Abu Dhabi October 11, 1978), p. 3.

The Role of Education 63

17. The present writer had an opportunity to witness such action on several occasions during her stay in the field. In one such case, Shaykh Zayid and Shaykha Fatima had received word that over a six-month period a number of female students had withdrawn from schools in several of the newly built Bedouin settlements on the outskirts of Abu Dhabi. Very quickly a delegation of women from the Ministry of Education and the Abu Dhabi Women's Society was assembled and sent to the schools and homes of these girls to find out why they left school and to try to re-enroll them. Had this personal interest not been taken, these girls would most likely have never returned to school and the same fate would probably have awaited their sisters. However, through the initiative of the ruling family, the problems were discovered and discussed and solutions are now in the making. And, through the urging of Shaykh Zayid and Shaykha Fatima, most of the girls' parents agreed to send them back to school.

18. Each school is assigned one social worker per 500 students, according to school authorities interviewed.

19. According to data from the Ministry of Education, 2,764 nationals dropped out of school in the 1977-78 academic year. See 'School Drop-outs Total 5,038', *Emirates News* (Abu Dhabi, August 19, 1978), p. 3. Also, although exact figures could not be obtained for previous years, authorities at the Ministry of Education and Youth stated that more males than females left school each year; local school administrative personnel also confirmed this. For the year 1975-76 (the only year in which figures on the basis of sex were available but not according to nationality), boys represented 7 percent of the drop-out rate and girls 4 percent. The great bulk of the drop-outs were in the primary levels (1,583 out of 2,354 males and 782 out of 1,116 female drop-outs) suggesting perhaps problems in teacher qualifications. Robert Mertz *(Education and Manpower*, p. 156) made note of this aspect of the drop-out rate in 1972 and felt the low quality of teachers at this level was the main reason for the high drop-out rate. Reasons given by the Ministry of Education were work, migration outside the UAE, marriage, death and illness. *Annual Statistical Abstract*, p. 300.

20. Several parents and students complained about the severe methods used, especially by some of the foreign teachers. The UAE depends very heavily on foreign instructors (91 percent) since it still does not have enough of its own, and this may be the main reason for the high drop-out rate at the primary level. Most of the instructors at this level are of low quality because the preparation of primary school teachers is considered of less importance, in general. This is not only a problem in the UAE but throughout the Arab World (See Mohammed El-Ghannam, *Education in the Arab Region (UNESCO* Pub., Paris, 1971), p. 19) and needs to be rectified. Only 24 percent of primary school teachers in the UAE have a university degree as opposed to 88 percent for the secondary level (Ministry of Education, *Educational Abstract, 1976-1977*, pp. 69-70).

21. Ministry of Education and Youth, *Annual Report of the Social Services Department, 1975-76* (in Arabic) (Abu Dhabi), pp. 21-2.

22. Based on interviews with headmistresses at various UAE schools.

23. See Table 3 in Appendix B.

24. Ester Boserup, *Integration of Women in Development: Why, When, How* (United Nations Development Programme, New York, May 1975), p. 29.

25. According to Ministry of Education data, female enrollment in the sciences at secondary level has been, on the average over a 5-year time period, 15 percent lower than that of the males in the sciences, and the gap has been even wider during these last two years. *Educational Abstract, 1976-1977*, p. 40.

26. Kindergarten schools began opening in 1968, and there are now nearly 4,000 children enrolled in these, all of which are coeducational. *Educational Abstract, 1976-1977*, pp. 13, 28.

64 *The Role of Education*

27. The information in this and the two preceding paragraphs is based on interviews with school administrators in 4 towns where co-ed schools are located. There are now 23 co-ed schools throughout the UAE, serving 1,483 children, 97 percent of whom are primary level students and, of these, 62 percent are male. *Educational Abstract, 1976-1977*, pp. 21-2.

28. *Educational Abstract, 1976-1977*, p. 53.

29. Woodsmall, *Moslem Women Enter A New World*, p. 248.

30. Students from outside the UAE must have completed through grade 9 in order to enter the nursing school. In time it is expected that the entrance requirements will become stricter for all.

31. Ras Al-Khaymah had a one-year nursing program from 1973-75 but it was discontinued. The local government is now planning on setting up a nursing school, as are Sharjah and Dubay, in the near future.

32. Abu Dhabi's nursing school was the first such school in the Gulf at the time it opened in 1972.

33. 'How Do We Develop Nursing in Our Country?' (in Arabic), *Al-Ittihad* (Abu Dhabi, February 6, 1978), p. 3. Also, the bulk of the information here comes from interviews with the directress of the nursing school and a group of nursing students.

34. Figures beyond grade 6 could not be obtained (suggesting a low drop-out level), but this was the comment of several administrators and school directors.

35. Female enrollment in secondary school has increased by 11 percent since 1972; females then comprised 34 percent of the total secondary school enrollment and now this figure is over 45 percent of the total enrollment. *Educational Abstract, 1976-1977*, p. 40.

36. 'Women's Lib-Kuwait Style', *The Middle East* (May 1978), p. 83.

37. 'Focus on Saudi Arabia – For Women, Education and Luxury Bring Mixed Blessing', *International Herald Tribune* (Paris, February 1978), pp. 10-15.

38. 'Education – Where Should the Money be Spent?' *Events* (January 13, 1978), p. 39.

39. According to my interviews with university staff members and 'University a Pillar of Unity', *Emirates News* (Abu Dhabi, October 16, 1978), p. 3.

40. Mertz, *Education and Manpower*, p. 157.

41. The first two females ever to attend college were part of Sharjah's first secondary school graduating class in 1964, which was made up of a total of four girls. These two attended university in Egypt and graduated with social science degrees in 1968. As of 1975, the number of UAE females studying abroad reached 204 and, by 1976-77, the government had 267 female scholarship students in foreign countries. The number of male students during these time periods were 1,032 and 1,298, respectively. These figures show a slightly higher percentage increase in the number of females studying abroad over the number of male students for this two-year time period. UAE Ministry of Information and Culture, *Facts and Figures* (1976), p. 51; and UAE Ministry of Education and Youth, *Educational Abstract, 1976-1977*, pp. 100-1.

42. *Facts and Figures* (1976), p. 53; *Educational Abstract 1976-1977*, p. 101. Males went from 153 in 1975 to 349 in 1977 and females increased from 12 to 26.

43. Based on my interviews with UAE college graduates and UAE women still studying in the West, there have been no problems of readjustment for those returning home after studying abroad. Perhaps it is still too early to tell since only one or two UAE women have so far completed a full four years of study in the USA or Britain, but most feel there will be no problems for them or their peers because they understand and respect their culture and traditions and prefer them to Western ways. All they wish to adopt from the West are skills and knowledge –

The Role of Education 65

not cultural habits.

44. The number of female adult education centers has grown from 18 centers with 1,466 participants in 1972 to 29 centers with 2,746 participants in 1976. *Facts and Figures* (1976), p. 55. The incentive for a male participating in such a program is that he will very likely obtain a better job if he is literate, so the male participation rate is obviously going to be higher for this reason, especially.

45. Among all the women interviewed, the overwhelming majority had attained a level of education equal to or lower than that of their husbands; it is rare to find marriages where the wife is better educated than the husband.

46. This was the most common phrase mentioned when the writer asked UAE women how they felt men perceived educated women.

47. A group of former evening school graduates are now enrolled at Al'Ain University – all are young, single women, this according to my interviews with Evening Program Directresses.

48. Older women (past 30) rarely continue beyond the level of attaining literacy, mainly because they feel embarrassed by their age; this attitude is slowly changing though.

49. At several schools, the problem of pregnancy was brought up by the head-mistresses since it forced some of the married students to drop out of the program for a while, but they usually returned after 2-3 months and were prepared by final exam time.

50. Vincent Sheean, *Faisal: The King and His Kingdom* (University Press of Arabia, England, 1975), pp. 104-5.

51. The view put forward in one UN study in 1975 was that Gulf officials in general look upon the issue of women's rights as being 'insignificant'. See 'Persian Gulf Women Find Less Freedom Now', *Christian Science Monitor* (July 2, 1975), p.1. In light of the efforts of such rulers as Shaykh Zayid, this is a very unfair accusation to make.

52. It might be noted that there are a total of forty private schools in the area, catering mainly to children of the expatriate community, and, of their total of 9,545 students in primary through secondary levels, only 253 are UAE nationals, or 2.6 percent. *Educational Abstract, 1976-1977*, pp. 5, 114, 121.

53. This is in reference to Schacht's article, 'Pre-Islamic Background and Early Development of Jurisprudence', pp. 34-5, which claims that, once a notion prevails among the Arabs, 'what had shortly before been an innovation then becomes the thing to do, a thing hallowed by precedent and tradition, a sunna'.

4 THE ROLE OF WOMEN IN THE UAE ECONOMY

Women as Economic Actors: A Modern Need or an Islamic Right?

The effects of veiling and seclusion were also to be felt by women in their attempts to exercise economic freedom. Even though the Qur'an strengthened the economic position of women, because of local traditions forcing women to remain within the limits of the home it was very difficult for them to exercise their economic rights. It is obvious that in the pre- and early Islamic periods women did enjoy economic freedom, and it is well known that the Prophet's wife, Khadija, was a highly successful businesswoman. The Prophet himself was greatly concerned with this issue, and there is much Qur'anic legislation referring to women's right to inherit as well as bequeath.[1] Daughters are entitled to their portion, as are wives and mothers, each according to her position in the family.[2] They are free to spend or invest this money or property without approval of the closest male relative, and a husband cannot coerce his wife into giving him money. Even among poor couples it is uncommon for a wife to confuse her property or money with that of her husband's, as there is no community of property between them. The fact that the *mahr* is also to be given to the woman for her own personal use and not to her father is another example of Islam's support for economic independence for women.

In many parts of the Muslim world, women no longer receive their inheritance shares as guaranteed by Islam. Families who did not want their wealth divided and spread apart by the portions given married daughters, who move away from home and take their share with them, simply stopped abiding by the laws. Beginning with the Abbasid period, an intricate *waqf* or mortmain system was devised so as to deny the descendants of daughters from benefiting from the Qur'anic rights to succession. Any property that was previously owned by women as a result of inheritance would pass into the hands of the state upon their death, rather than to their descendants. In this way, the old Arab patriarchal system was strengthened, in direct opposition to Islamic law. Male family heads now had a 'legal' reason for not bequeathing property to their female relatives, i.e., the excuse that the property would eventually be confiscated by the state.[3] And, over the years, the practice of excluding females from inheritance has become firmly rooted.

66

The Role of Women in the UAE Economy

Employment outside of the home is viewed honorably by Islam, and there is even a saying by the Prophet that 'the most blessed earning is that which a person gains from his own labor'.[4] However, because of the tradition of veiling and seclusion, women have obviously been limited in their choice of professions. In addition, men have generally been opposed to their womenfolk taking wage-earning jobs because this would give them the economic independence to which they are entitled under Islam, but to which men are opposed. Women have, however, continued to work through the centuries. To the outsider, it would appear as though there were no opportunities for women to assume wage employment, and, indeed, the percentages of Arab women in the wage-earning sectors were extremely low up to 10 or 20 years ago. However, these figures failed to take into account the fact that many women were independently employed in the private sectors. In many areas of the Arab world, women raised, for income, chickens or lambs, while others sold goat's cheese and milk, wove or embroidered fabric and sewed clothing. In addition, women were employed as agricultural laborers, midwives, religious instructors, domestic workers, or healers of sick women and children.

Once women attained the right to equal educational opportunities, which started the process of bringing them out of seclusion, the next step was entrance into the modern economic sector, and, since the early 1900s, women's participation in this sector has been growing slowly but steadily. The developing countries of the Arab world cannot afford to allow the resources of one-half of the population to go untapped, so, in many areas, women have been encouraged to work in the public sectors. That is not to say that women entered the labor force only because men gave them permission to do so. Rather, it was a combination of factors which prompted female entry into many traditionally male fields. The most important of these factors was that the women themselves became aware, through their newly acquired schooling, that their previous restrictions were man-made and not religious obligations. So they felt they had the right to work in any field they chose. Indeed, national economic policies furthered their cause, as rapid modernization was, and continues to be, the goal of all these states, and every educated citizen is needed to meet this goal. It remains, however, an accepted fact that a woman's right to gainful employment has existed since the earliest days of Islam and is guaranteed by the Qur'an. This right is not therefore a twentieth-century innovation, but an Islamic tradition, well defended by the verse: 'Unto men a fortune from that which they have earned, and unto women a fortune from that which

68 The Role of Women in the UAE Economy

they have earned.' (Qur'an IV:32).

Economic Investment and Employment Opportunities Available to UAE Women in the Past

Contrary to the fact that, throughout most parts of the Muslim East, women were denied their inheritance rights,[5] women of the Gulf area have always received their assured shares as designated by the Qur'an. Thus, even during the period when pearling and fishing were the primary forms of economic activity in this part of the Arabian Peninsula, it was not unusual to find that women owned many of the ships that went to sea. In addition, some of the trading merchants were female, but they have always conducted their business through men acting on their behalf, and continue to do so. Not only did women inherit money, which could be invested, but also many of the ruling families' womenfolk were recipients of large parcels of land. Once oil was discovered and land began selling at a premium throughout the UAE area, many of these women became quite wealthy through the development of their real estate. Obviously, though, such women were in the minority. For most women, life was quite a hardship, and trying to survive economically without a husband or older brother would have been extremely difficult in the pre-oil wealth period. Life was no less difficult for men, either, as many were forced to take pearl-diving jobs, which entailed a great deal of physical danger and meant separation from their families for months at a time while they were at sea.

Pearling reached its peak just before the First World War and, after this, the market was flooded with Japanese cultured pearls. Except for Dubay, which was active in the world gold trade and later became a very prosperous trade center, and Sharjah, which benefited from its proximity to Dubay, the Gulf states sank into poverty after the decline of the pearling industry. Fishing then became the most important industry for these small states and has continued to remain so for 'Ajman and Umm al-Qaywayn. Ras Al-Khaymah had some farming activity, while Abu Dhabi's people existed as desert pastoralists or fishermen, and Fujayrah's inhabitants traded dried lemons and tobacco.[6]

For those women who needed to provide an income for themselves and their children, the opportunities were very limited indeed. Some raised chickens, sheep or goats and sold eggs, meat, cheese and milk door-to-door. Others worked as seamstresses, healers, Qur'anic instructors and some were even employed as hairstylers. Bedouin women, in addition to these employment activities, would sell woolen cloth they

The Role of Women in the UAE Economy

had woven, and honey.[7] Income-earning opportunities were only slightly more varied for women of this area than for men.

It was not until after the discovery of oil in Abu Dhabi that development plans of any kind could be formulated as the area was so impoverished. Shaykh Zayid's new leadership ushered in the first development plan ever designed (1968–72) for Abu Dhabi.[8] Even during the period before the union, Shaykh Zayid not only built up his own state, but immediately began pouring money into the treasuries of other neighboring shaykhdoms so as also to contribute to their development.[9] The prosperity that followed was to improve the wage-earning capacity not only of men, but of women too.

Employment Opportunities for UAE Women Today: The Public Sector

The segregation of men and women into different social spheres paved the way, throughout the Middle East, for women's entry into the professions of teaching and medicine, in particular. Teaching has always been considered the most honorable occupation for women in the Muslim East, and a broad range of opportunities in this field continue to be available because men are barred from girls' schools and the supply of local teachers is still limited and characterized by low levels of skill acquisition. Because, in many regions, male doctors cannot treat females, opportunities are also great in the field of medicine. But the area has yet to produce a sufficient supply of female doctors and there is still dependency on foreign female physicians in many parts of the Arab world.

In the teaching and medical professions, the question of work and honor is not an issue; from this fact stems the acceptance and popularity of these fields. When an employment position entailed exposing a female to men, thereby posing a possible threat to family honor, the chances of a woman's family permitting her to enter such a working situation were slim. The idea of a woman having to take orders from a man and being under his control also kept women out of many job areas. Now, however, such barriers have begun to break down, and women throughout the Middle East have started entering professions once reserved exclusively for men.[10]

According to Nadia Youssef, in almost all developing countries, 'evidence shows that the least resistance to female employment currently is expressed at the professional level', and well-educated women are entering traditionally male-dominated fields.[11] In the Arabian Gulf area, it has only been in the last 10-20 years that women have been allowed to work at all but, to date, the greatest headway has been made

70 The Role of Women in the UAE Economy

at the professional level, albeit mainly in the fields of education, health and social work, primarily because sex segregation is still strongly practiced in most parts of the Gulf.[12]

The positions held by women in the United Arab Emirates are concentrated solely in the professions. Employment in government ministries is considered most acceptable for UAE women. However, outside of the Ministries of Health, Education, and Labor and Social Affairs, the number of local women employed is extremely limited.[13] These restrictions are a result of social attitudes and not government policy. On the contrary, the government has, from the start, embarked on a policy which would encourage female participation in the labor force. Shaykh Zayid has also spoken out in support of women's involvement in national development, and he has urged educated women not to allow their skills to go to waste. Many Prophetic sayings and Qur'anic verses are referred to as proof that wage-earning employment is not forbidden by Islam nor considered shameful. The kind of official support extended to UAE women to encourage them to work is difficult to find in other Arab countries, not to mention in many Western countries, where women are still battling for employment opportunities equal to those available for men. UAE women have gained access to various occupations at different levels of employment. Although most of the select, high-level positions are reserved for university graduates, in several UAE ministries women are admitted with few or no qualifications. As explained by one official, this is because every individual woman willing to work must be given the opportunity, so that, in time, as more and more females join the paid labor force, their participation will become the norm and conservative families will be less reluctant to permit their daughters to work. What is most important is that women get out and participate in various types of employment, and, later, as their numbers and skills increase, the adherence to strict requirements concerning job qualifications can be implemented. In a number of offices, on-the-job training of local women by foreign professionals has been proceeding quite satisfactorily. Indeed, in several cases local women have already taken charge of various departments within certain government offices.

The history of local women's participation in the formal sector dates back to 1964, before the formation of the UAE, when the Kuwayt office hired two women to teach at schools in Sharjah.[14] These two women were among the four secondary school graduates of Sharjah's first female graduating class. As of 1977, out of a total of 2,357 female instructors employed by the Ministry of Education, 199 or 8.4 percent

The Role of Women in the UAE Economy 71

were local women, and, of the administrative staff, 128 out of 551 female administrators, or 23 percent, were local women.[15] At present, there is a strong preference for local women to take on the top positions in school administration. Therefore, after one or two years of teaching, a woman is usually promoted to assistant headmistress or even headmistress of a school. This is the case in all states except Sharjah and Dubay. Here more female instructors are available because of the teaching institute, so the competition for the top positions is keener, as there are more qualified women than administrative positions. This is only true at the primary level because, throughout the Emirates, there is a shortage of local teachers and administrators for the preparatory and secondary levels as teachers for these levels are required to have university degrees. There are local women heading the Ministry of Education's Social Services Department, and there are several women working as secretaries for the female administrators in this section. However, on the whole, clerical work is left to men, a common phenomenon throughout the Middle East. Unlike the West, where such occupations are reserved for women, because of the need for women in the Muslim East to work in a secluded atmosphere, away from the public eye and especially the eyes of men, the clerical field was closed to most Muslim women from the start of women's involvement in the labor force. Although increasing numbers of Arab women are entering the clerical field, it will still be a while before the stigma attached to it disappears.[16]

The Ministry of Labor and Social Affairs attracts the second-largest group of local women (the Ministry of Education being the most popular). Local women began working here when the Ministry was established in 1972. The Abu Dhabi branch of the Ministry has no local women employees, but the offices in Dubay and Sharjah employ approximately 10 women as social workers in the local offices and at the women's social center in Sharjah. All of the local women received training from the Ministry as none had previous experience in social work. Social work is still a new field, however, and only now does it have a bit more prestige than it did a few years ago, because of the services it provides. The job of the female social worker entails visiting and interviewing female applicants for social welfare aid residing in the northern Emirates. Although these employees' superiors are all males, their parents have encouraged them to stay on with the Ministry because they have seen that they are providing a necessary service. Most of the women are single and are wisely pursuing their studies in the adult literacy programs. Since many of them did not have the opportunity to finish secondary level before beginning work, they have now made this

72 The Role of Women in the UAE Economy

their primary goal. A number of the women expressed their awareness that, in time, they expected to be replaced by university-educated social workers. So they see it as their responsibility to try and acquire as much education as possible now, and some even have plans of pursuing sociology at the university level at Al-'Ain.[17]

In the medical field, the opportunities available to local women have yet to be taken advantage of. The UAE has yet to produce its first female physician, so there is total dependency on foreign female doctors. And since women can only be treated by other women, the demand for women doctors is very high. Because of the low social and moral esteem extended to nursing in the UAE and throughout the Middle East as a whole, since this job is often associated with servants' work, it will take time to bring about a change in attitudes. As a nurse must come in contact with men, an additional impediment to women's entrance into the field is posed.

Local women first entered the field of nursing, albeit as nurse's aides, in 1964, when, as a form of assistance in the area, before oil wealth or the union of the shaykhdoms, the Kuwayti government built a 60-bed hospital in Dubay in 1963. Hospital representatives were sent to schools throughout the area to encourage females to enter the nursing field primarily because there was a great need for Arabic-speaking nurses. Local women first began working in the Kuwayt Hospital in 1964, when five young women from Sharjah were among the first to be employed, and they received training as nurse's aides by the professional medical staff. The Kuwayti government even offered to finance the formal training of these women so that they could become registered nurses if their parents would allow them to study nursing abroad, but the families refused. Even after the establishment of the nursing school in Abu Dhabi, which has had its own share of problems recruiting students,[18] parents still refused to allow their daughters to board away from home. The best and only solution for the northern Emirates, therefore, is to build a local nursing school so women can be properly trained.

When the Emirates united in 1971, one of the first projects of the new Ministry of Health was to recruit young women for the increasing numbers of state hospitals being built. From Sharjah, again, came the largest number of recruits (eight), and women began to receive training as nurse's aides for Sharjah's hospital in 1975.[19]

The main complaint of the nurse's aides interviewed was that they greatly desired formal schooling, but that the Ministry of Health was slow in responding to their needs. The consensus was that, once a local

The Role of Women in the UAE Economy

nursing school was established, more local women would be encouraged to enter nursing. Many women leave their positions as nurse's aides after a year or two because of the lack of proper training and because of boredom with their jobs once the limited skills have been acquired. Since there is only a handful of local women in each hospital, the Ministry of Health can hardly afford to lose many of these women. The nursing school being built in Sharjah is now, however, nearing completion, so this problem should soon be solved. It is the intention of all of the present nurse's aides to return to school and receive formal nurse's training so they may become full-fledged nurses, rather than assistants to the foreign staff. Hopefully, in this way, too, prestige will be accorded to the field as women will have degrees to vouch for the seriousness and importance of their work.[20]

Women have also been attracted to the field of radio and television broadcasting. The first local female to be employed as a radio broadcaster was a young woman from Sharjah. She was recruited by the British government to work at the radio station of the Trucial Oman Scouts (predecessor of the UAE Defense Force), which was opened in Dubay in 1967. The station was later taken over by the Ministry of Information and Culture when it was established at the time of the formation of the UAE in 1971. Since that time, the Ministry of Information and Culture has continued to recruit local women to work as news-broadcasters at stations throughout the UAE.

By 1972, there were three local women employed at Abu Dhabi's radio and television broadcasting stations – announcing the news, helping to organize children's and variety programs and even acting in short plays televised for viewer entertainment during the month of Ramadan. The local people's reaction to seeing women from their own country on television was not, at first, entirely supportive. Many of the older generation still consider it shameful for a woman to show her face on television, before thousands of people. However, many of the younger women expressed gratitude for the courage of these women in entering broadcasting, since their example has encouraged other women to take jobs outside the home. There are also television and radio broadcasters in Dubay and Sharjah (one in each). Most of them have not completed secondary schooling but the Ministry provides a six-month training course for all its new recruits. All the women enjoyed good relations with their co-workers and stated that the male co-workers were especially supportive of their positions. Abu Dhabi's radio station already has one female supervisor, in the programming division, an indication that women are taken seriously by the Ministry of Infor-

74 The Role of Women in the UAE Economy

mation and Culture.[21]

To handle such work as the searching of female travelers at airports, or those under arrest, the Ministry of the Interior began hiring local women in 1973 as part of the local police units. Their numbers remained limited (four women were employed in 1973 and ten in 1975) until 1977, when it was decided that many more women inspectors were needed to handle a variety of new problems. An active campaign was thus launched to recruit women through the local police units. Abu Dhabi's police force succeeded in recruiting 24 women from the area as part of its first female unit, while Dubay's police force recruited 18 local women.[22] On completing a four-month training course, the same course given to male recruits, the first unit of policewomen graduated from Dubay in April 1978 and from Abu Dhabi in July 1978.[23] The women have been posted to various police centers, and their duties include criminal investigations concerning women and juveniles, airport searches of women, administering driving license examinations for women, and working with imprisoned women. Many of the new recruits are married, and all are relatively young (20-25 years of age). Although completion of secondary school level is not required, many are participating in adult literacy programs because rank is based on one's educational level. Therefore, if a female has a secondary school degree, she automatically becomes an officer; otherwise, promotions are received on the basis of seniority and merit. There are already plans to send the first group of female officer-trainees to Jordan for a three-month course in specialized officer training. When these women return as officers, they will then assume most of the responsibilities involved in training new recruits, a job which has so far been handled by male officers only. It is hoped that more families will allow their daughters to join local police forces once female officers are fully in charge of the training and supervision of the policewomen.

As previously mentioned, clerical positions are rarely ceded to women throughout the Middle East because of the practice of sex segregation, and in this tradition the UAE is not an exception. There are very few local women working in clerical or administrative positions in any government ministry because of fears of violating morality taboos. The Ministry of Education, as earlier stated, has one or two local female secretaries working under local female directresses; the Ministry of Information and Culture has hired female secretaries for several of the broadcasting stations; and the Ministry of the Interior has hired women to serve as administrative assistants in some of the local police centers from 1973. In addition, some of the hospitals in Abu Dhabi, Sharjah

The Role of Women in the UAE Economy

and Dubay have hired local females as clerks and secretaries since 1972, but their numbers at each hospital rarely exceed three. Nor is it likely that the socially stigmatizing aspect of clerical work will soon disappear. So male secretaries from other parts of the Middle East will continue to be recruited to fill these positions since not enough local men are available or would be attracted to this field.

Interest in other fields such as law, politics, engineering or journalism is growing at a much slower pace than interest in teaching or social work, for example, because these are areas that require higher education and much experience. Even those women who have the necessary educational qualifications find it difficult to secure a job in these fields as many parents are opposed to their daughters entering predominantly male-controlled occupations. Because the first UAE female law graduate comes from a prominent family, she is not permitted to join the Ministry of Justice for fear of dishonoring her family. Since no other local women are employed at the Ministry, her entry might have encouraged other women to follow her example, but this first step will have to be taken by some other law school graduate in the future. The Abu Dhabi National Oil Company hired its first female petroleum engineer in 1977, the first local woman to work at the Ministry of Petroleum. Her family's apprehensions were allayed when her brother took on a similar position in her department, but what is important is that she is able to use her skills on a related job, instead of having to shelve her knowledge in the hope that the time may come when she can use her skills and not fear social stigmatization, as suffered by some female professionals. The Ministry of Foreign Affairs added two local women to its professional staff as of November 1977 – one is stationed in Abu Dhabi and the other is at the UAE embassy in Kuwayt. In all of these cases, as pioneer women in the pursuit of these fields, a great challenge and risk were involved. The sooner women spread themselves out in a variety of fields, the faster will the status of all women rise – not to mention national output.[24]

Employment and Investment Opportunities for UAE Women Today: The Private Sector

Employment opportunities for UAE women outside of government ministries is unheard of. Clerical or administrative positions in private businesses are not considered suitable jobs for women in segregated societies, for the obvious reason that they would be under the authority of strange men. The same holds true for domestic service occupations; no UAE woman would ever work as a servant in a private home, as

76   The Role of Women in the UAE Economy

exposing herself to male household members would bring dishonor upon herself and her family. Today, all domestic service positions are filled by expatriates, primarily Indians, Pakistanis, Egyptians and a growing number of Filipinos, Sudanese and Sri Lankans. Whatever manufacturing industries there are are also totally off-limits to local women. These industries, too, depend entirely on expatriate labor, and mostly male laborers, because there are not enough local men to fill these jobs. Even if there were sufficient numbers of local people to work in such industries as food, beverages, printing, chemicals, petroleum or machinery, women would still be excluded, unless the work was of a traditional handicraft-type nature and could be worked on in the home. Nor is work in trade or commerce socially permitted because it would expose a woman to a number of strangers. The position of a salesgirl is particularly taboo because, as several groups of women explained, it would be like putting oneself on public display, and the opportunity for strange men to speak with a woman and thus possibly dishonor her would be great. Therefore, while work in a government ministry is easily justified by most people – on the grounds that one is thus providing a public service, helping the nation to grow and develop – work in private industries is not considered justifiable at all. This is mainly because private sector work would not directly serve the nation; there is therefore no real need for the job, and it would unnecessarily expose a female to an unlimited number of strange men.

The investment opportunities for women in the private sector, unlike the employment opportunities in this sector, are quite extensive. If a woman has money or property of her own, she is free to invest it as she chooses without fear of dishonoring her family, as women have traditionally been involved in this type of business. Many female members of wealthy and ruling families have long held title to pieces of land which were acquired primarily through inheritance and which they are now developing into modern building sites and renting to other business contractors. Many women are also involved in trade – ranging from automobiles to clothing shops and jewelry stores. There are also many women who buy from one to dozens of taxicabs and rent them out to men, who drive the cars for them at a profit (i.e., depending on how much business they register on their meters each week, a percentage of that is their profit). Otherwise, a woman may choose to buy shares in a family business, or put her money into stocks bought on the open market. In all of these cases, however, the woman herself will not appear in any front office, or in any but a very few business meetings, because of local traditions regarding segregation. Rather, she will hire a

The Role of Women in the UAE Economy

man to be her representative for most business transactions. It is difficult to determine whether or not these women are fairly represented by their agents, and this is the main drawback to managing one's finances in this manner. There are also reports of expatriates who have served as representatives of local business people and who have slipped away with the entire financial reserves of local entrepreneurs. Of course, in a family-type business, there are no such problems, nor is the risk so great when one purchases stocks or rents buildings or cars, so these are the most favoured types of investment.[25]

Rights Rendered Women in the UAE Labor Force

Of those women participating in the labor force, Arab women have long had the rights that Western women have been struggling to achieve for years. Equal pay for men and women performing the same jobs, the most important of these rights, has still not been fully implemented in the United States nor in most European countries.[26] Throughout the Arab World, and in the UAE in particular, equal pay for equal work has been a long-standing tradition. Arab women are also treated equally with men in regard to working hours, sick leave, holiday leave, weekly day off, reasons for dismissal, and so on. In addition, most individual Arab states have passed labor legislation which includes provisions for mother and child welfare, as well as maternity leave, sickness due to childbirth, nursing hours and nurseries.[27] In this regard, the UAE grants leave for childbirth without determining the day when the leave begins, thus allowing the decision to be made by each individual woman, a policy which is in conformity with the labor standards of the International Labour Office.[28] Not only is pay for maternity leave and sick leave guaranteed by law in the UAE, but among a new set of civil service amendments signed into law on May 26, 1978 was one granting Muslim females fully paid leave of four months and ten days should their husbands pass away.[29] Through the implementation of such labor legislation, the UAE government is helping and encouraging the woman to take on the role of worker, as well as wife and mother, by guaranteeing her special rights so that she can handle home and employment responsibilities at the same time.

Effect of Women's Employment on Family Life

As education of females has an effect on marriage and family life, primarily in the form of delaying marriage and, perhaps, reducing the number of children born, so employment of females has its effects on marriage and family life. In the case of the UAE, it is still too soon to

78   The Role of Women in the UAE Economy

measure these effects, but it may be helpful to see what the general outcomes have been in most societies.

The first consistent effect has been a lowering of birth rates when women are ensured the right to equal work and equal pay. Of course, there are many factors to take into consideration here, such as which sectors of the economy women are employed in and whether on a full- or part-time basis, the availability of children's nurseries, whether women are working for financial gain or for the psychological benefits, and so on.[30]

Female employment, when it is pursued out of economic necessity, is often viewed as an obstacle to spending time with one's children. However, when the woman is of a high socio-economic bracket and therefore is working not out of financial need, but more for personal gratification, because she enjoys her work and feels more fulfilled by it, she is psychologically better able to deal with her home responsibilities.[31] The most important question concerning women's employment is exactly what effect it has on the raising of children. However, it is only in recent years that the number of young married women in the labor force has shown an upward trend, in both developed and developing countries, and studies that have been conducted have, so far, 'failed to confirm the widespread belief that employment of mothers of young children adversely affects the next generation'.[32] If it is true that there are no adverse effects, many women may change their attitudes about working, both in developed and developing countries.[33]

An important factor to keep in mind when studying the characteristics of employed women in the UAE is that none of the working women have to work out of economic necessity. If a woman has no male relatives to support her, she may rely on the government's generous welfare system, which allows no woman or man to go without the basic necessities of life. Rather, UAE woman work out of a sense of duty to their country and a need for self-fulfillment.[34] It should, therefore, be easier for most women to assume roles both of mother and of worker because they are aware that they are not forced to work.[35] In addition, with the increase of child-care centers and the ready availability of domestic help, a UAE woman is even more capable of combining the two roles.

A last important effect to consider is the possible further delay in marriage caused by female employment, as occurs when there is female education. A possible outgrowth of this may be that at the professional levels especially, where a greater sense of financial independence and social satisfaction is felt, employment may even be viewed as an alter-

The Role of Women in the UAE Economy 79

native to marriage.[36] This kind of attitude would not, however, very easily take root in most Muslim societies. More women may be forced to work once economic demands become too great for the men to handle alone, and financial constraints may lower the number of children women choose to have, causing a change in some values, but the institution of marriage will itself remain strong throughout Muslim societies.[37]

Conclusion

On looking at the occupational areas UAE women tend to concentrate in, the social stigma attached to private sector employment and to any positions where a woman is on view to the public is clearly the reason for women's preference for public sector jobs. This practice continues in spite of the fact that the Islamic religion designates no special jobs for women and the fact that the UAE government has officially supported the participation of women in all economic sectors at the public and private level.

Two very strong tribal traditions as well as Islamic laws observed in the UAE are the right of women to inheritance and the right of women to control their own earnings. UAE women are completely free to enter independently into investment opportunities, and many do so. Regardless of the fact that a UAE businesswoman is usually represented by a male in most transactions, she reserves to herself full control of major decision making. For the employed woman, her income is also hers alone, and any contributions made to the family's budget are purely voluntary, as the man is considered completely responsible for financially providing for his family. The economic independence traditionally enjoyed by women of this area should prove an additional incentive to women's increased participation in the labor force, as it already has proven to be an incentive for women's growing involvement in the private investment sector.

Trying to change centuries-old stereotypes is a difficult task in any society, and when so much emphasis is put on the wife-mother roles of women, as is the case in Muslim societies, this task is even more formidable. That is not to say that the significance of these roles must be diminished, as they are extremely important and revered by Islam, rather, the roles must be broadened so that, in addition to viewing herself as wife and mother, the UAE woman can also see herself in the roles of student, teacher, worker, or leader. The educational and employment opportunities now available in the Emirates can help bring about this change, as similar opportunities have been the catalyst of de-stereo-

80 The Role of Women in the UAE Economy

typing and increased role assumption of other Gulf women, and Arab women in general. Change will not come overnight and life will continue to be difficult for the single woman but, at least, if a woman is unmarried, whether by choice or fate, other career opportunities outside that of home-maker will be open to her.

Finally, while it may be true that, in Muslim societies especially, a woman does not feel the need to be economically self-sufficient because there is security in the knowledge that one's male relative will always be responsible for her, not all countries or persons are equally well endowed, and women have been forced to raise families alone since earliest times. This attitude may therefore apply today to women of the upper class in many Muslim countries, and the wealthier states especially, but for most middle-class females the desire to work is high.[38] When UAE women were questioned concerning their willingness to work, assuming they were in a situation where they would never be wanting for money, the most common response was that a woman works to gain status and a sense of self-worth and not for economic reasons. As mentioned earlier, great pride is expressed in the fact that these women are applying their skills toward making their society stronger and more prosperous.

The fact that most UAE working women are concentrated in the so-called 'feminine' occupations relating to education, health and social planning should not be cause for discouragement as, surely, these areas, as much as any other, are badly in need of qualified local people. As one UN study has shown, women in many of these traditional occupations do often have the opportunity of reaching high positions, and in periods of unemployment there is a greater chance that they will remain employed in these sectors than if they are in male-dominated fields.[39] However, this is not to say that women should not be encouraged to enter areas traditionally dominated by men, too; and it is certain that women will begin to be more visible in other professional fields. The areas in which females are concentrating at the university level makes this an inevitable outcome.[40] Through official encouragement of women's educational and employment pursuits at all levels, and in all areas, the UAE has already shown that it has learned much from the mistakes of developed countries, which have, until very recently, done little to encourage their own women to enter 'male' fields.[41] That the situation of women in the UAE can only improve, as a result of the continual rise in educational level, along with social and economic development, is undoubted. Prospects for higher levels of participation in the labor force are clear, even though women's levels of

The Role of Women in the UAE Economy

representation are still very low.[42] The effect of local traditions regarding sex segregation is still considerable, and no woman would embark on a career without first consulting her family, and the male head in particular; but with each new generation, more and more flexibility will exist.[43] What is most important when one is examining the role of UAE women in the economy, whether as part of the public labor force or private investment sector, is that neither Islam nor government policy is keeping them from becoming economically active. The Islamic religion bestows economic freedom upon men and women, and UAE government officials have been quick and wise in pointing this out. In any case, when a woman is denied the right to exercise this freedom by family members, the blame lies on tradition, and not on religion or government policy. However, with the passing of time and through the effects of equal educational opportunities in particular, it is likely that tradition will wield less and less weight against the forces of modernization, and that women's quantitative as well as qualitative input into the economy will rise.

Notes

1. See, for example, Suras II:177, IV:11, 12, 7 and 32, in Appendix A.
2. For a thorough explanation of this, see Abu Zahra, 'Family Law', pp. 160-78.
3. P.M. Holt, A.K. Lambton and B. Lewis (eds), *The Cambridge History of Islam* (The University Press, Cambridge, 1970), vol. II, pp. 560-1.
4. This is one among many proverbs used by UAE officials to encourage women to work today.
5. For a discussion of this, see Baer, *Population and Society*, pp. 38-40.
6. Kevin Fenelon, *The UAE: An Economic and Social Survey* (Longman, London, 1976), pp. 59-72.
7. Based on my interviews with older women throughout the UAE.
8. 'Oil Production, Revenues and Economic Development', *The Economist*, QER Special no. 18 (1974), pp. 49-50.
9. John D. Anthony, *Arab States of the Lower Gulf: People, Politics Petroleum* (Middle East Institute, Washington, DC, 1975), p. 143.
10. For specific examples of this, see such studies as 'The UNESCO Report on the Relationship Between Educational Opportunities and Employment Opportunities for Women', pp. 71-92; and Ester Boserup, *Women's Role in Economic Development*, pp. 102-3.
11. Nadia Youssef, 'Women In Development: Urban Life and Labor' in Irene Tinker and Michel Bramsen (eds), *Women and World Development* (Overseas Development Council, Washington, DC, 1976), p. 73.
12. Ali Taki, *The Changing Status of the Bahraini Woman* (Oriental Press, Bahrayn, 1974), pp. 29-35; and 'Focus on Kuwait: Women, An Image of Modernity for Their Gulf Sisters', *International Herald Tribune* (Paris, February 1978), p. 2-S.

82 The Role of Women in the UAE Economy

13. See Appendix C, Table 1.

14. A note of possible interest is that none of the women presently in the public labor force had working mothers; some may have older sisters who work but, generally speaking, this is the first generation of formally employed women.

15. *Educational Abstract, 1976-1977*, pp. 62-3.

16. Nadia Youssef, *Women and Work in Developing Countries*, pp. 36-40.

17. According to my interviews with social workers in Dubay and Sharjah.

18. Refer back to pages 55-6 of this study.

19. The first five women from Sharjah to work as nurse's aides in 1968, as mentioned in the previous paragraph, were employed in Dubay and not Sharjah because it was still not acceptable for women to work in Sharjah's medical dispensary at that time. It was not until 1975 that girls from Sharjah began working in hospitals in Sharjah.

20. The information on nursing is based on my interviews with nurses's aides in four hospitals in Dubay and Sharjah. There are no local women employed as nurse's aides in the other northern Emirates because in those areas it is still not acceptable for women to enter this field.

21. Based on interviews with female Ministry employees in Abu Dhabi and Sharjah.

22. Based on interviews with members of Dubay's police force; also see, 'Police Department to Employ Women', *Emirates News* (March 20, 1978), p. 1.

23. 'Policewoman's Graduation', *Emirates News* (April 13, 1978); and 'Women Police End Course', *Emirates News* (July 26, 1978), p. 1.

24. Economist Arthur Lewis, as quoted in International Labour Office, *Equality of Opportunity and Treatment for Women Workers*, Report VIII (ILO, Geneva, 1975), p. 69.

25. This section is based primarily on interviews with businesswomen in Abu Dhabi, Ras Al-Khaymah and Sharjah.

26. R.B. Ginsburg, 'The Status of Women' in *The American Journal of Comparative Law*, vol. 20, no. 4 (Fall 1972), p. 587; and *The Status of Women in Arab Law in the Light of UN Conventions*, p. 82.

27. El-Sayed El-Tahry, 'The Working Woman in the Arab Homeland', in *International Women's News* (February 1978), p. 4.

28. Ibid., p. 5. Also, it might be noted that most Western countries have yet to provide such services. United Nations Report, *Participation of Women in the Economic and Social Development of their Countries* (New York), pp. 70-1.

29. 'President Signs Civil Service Amendments', *Emirates News* (Abu Dhabi, May 27, 1978), p. 1.

30. United Nations, *Status of Women and Family Planning* (United Nations Pub., New York, 1975), p. 45.

31. Ibid., p. 45.

32. Boserup, *Women's Role in Economic Development*, pp. 137-8.

33. Ibid., p. 138.

34. Based on my interviews with working women throughout the UAE.

35. This was proved in studies by the UN; women who work out of desire rather than need often handle their domestic responsibilities quite easily. *Status of Women and Family Planning*, p. 45.

36. *Status of Women and Family Planning*, p. 44.

37. If anything, women in the UAE, for example, would choose marriage over work, but that choice does not have to be made in most cases, since both can be pursued with little conflict. So long as men are willing to allow their wives to work, marriage conflicts will be minimal and the institution will remain intact. As shown by a UN study on men and women in Lebanon, men over 40, irrespective of social status or education, felt a woman's place was in the home; while men

The Role of Women in the UAE Economy

under 40 were in favor of equality of employment and education for men and women, primarily because they felt that a working wife was an economic asset because she helped meet household costs. (*Report on the Relationship Between Educational Opportunities and Employment Opportunities for Women*, p. 75.) Morroe Berger also makes note of a study on Egyptian women from which he infers that 'men are increasingly aware of the repressive character of traditional family life for women', and that young men, especially, want wives of equal educational level, for example, so that 'now proportionally more marriages begin with a greater measure of independence for the wife'. (Berger, *The Arab World*, pp. 133-4). In both of these analyses, it appears that men are reconciling these new changes in women's lives with the marriage situation, rather than seeking to keep women subordinate and, thereby, causing conflict and disharmony, and possibly even destroying their marriages.

38. Morroe Berger, *The Arab World*, pp. 256-7. Berger states that, according to a sociological study conducted on girls in Egypt, 'A generation ago the daughters of middle-class families were more emancipated than those of upper-class families, which were apparently rather conservative. Thus emancipation and education seem to have spread upward and downward from the middle class . . . it was the middle class that made the tentative but unmistakable move towards change.' Ruth Woodsmall's findings seem to concur with this conclusion in her study on Muslim women in general (see *Women and the New East*, p. 364), where she states that 'women of the middle class are now moving toward economic independence. The degree of free economic participation of women in the middle class in each country is directly related to the social freedom of women of that country.'

39. United Nations, *Report of the Interregional Meeting of Experts on the Integration of Women in Development* (UN, New York, 1973), p. 60.

40. See Appendix C, Table 2.

41. According to a survey conducted by the US Department of Health, Education and Welfare in 1976, American women continue to dominate areas such as home economics and library service, although progress has been made in the period from 1971-76 in fields such as agriculture and natural resources, and business and management. 'Women in the U.S. Slowly Entering "Male" Fields', *International Herald Tribune* (Paris, June 5, 1978), p. 5.

42. It could not be determined from available population figures exactly what percentage of local women are of working age and what percentage of the female working population is of local or expatriate origin. If one assumed that there are approximately 450 local women employed in the public sector (based on Appendix C, Table 1), then they comprise 7.4 percent of the total number of females active in the labor force, and 0.15 percent of the entire economically active population (which includes nationals and non-nationals). *Annual Statistical Abstract* (1977), pp. 46-7.

43. Among the women I interviewed, it was the older women (especially those over 25 years of age) who most felt that men disapproved of women working, while the majority of younger women (married and single) stated that men supported the right of women to work; an indication that age has an effect on one's attitudes.

5 THE ROLE OF GOVERNMENTAL AND NON-GOVERNMENTAL ORGANIZATIONS IN IMPROVING THE STATUS OF WOMEN IN THE UAE

Combining Islamic Ritual with the Pragmatic Needs of a Developing Society

UAE development planners have included women in their designs since the formation of the union in 1971. However, had it not been for the strong support of some very key local figures, the progress made to date, through giving women special attention at the early stages of development, might not have occurred for a very long time. In all societies, no matter what the efforts of local people, without the required government assistance in such areas as education, social welfare and health, basic needs cannot be met. In the UAE, the official goal is to meet women's needs as soon as possible.

Without the participation of 50 percent of its citizenry, the UAE will remain helplessly dependent on continued expatriate assistance as the backbone of its labor force. Another important factor to be kept in mind is that oil is a non-renewable resource, which means the UAE will not have this income to rely on forever. Therefore, alternative sources of income must be found and nurtured very soon. This effort also requires the input of every capable member of UAE society, starting from now. While developing states are quick to begrudge oil-exporting states their short-lived prosperity, forgetting the centuries of decay and hardship the citizens of most of these states have endured, the memories of these people and their rulers are not so short. There is a feeling of urgency about pressing ahead and establishing substitutes for the days when oil is depleted. For this reason, any conflicts between Islam as interpreted by local traditions and the demands of modernization must be reconciled. The greatest of these conflicts is the position of women. Both Islam and modernization support the notion of freedom for women, while local traditions do not. However, over the past seven years, ruling families, government agencies and independent organizations have made, and continue to make, much progress in seeing that women are bestowed the rights due them by Islam, and thus the race towards modernization is not needlessly slowed down.

A major difficulty faced by local UAE officials lay, and continues to lie, in getting the women themselves involved in improving their own

The Role of Governmental and Non-governmental Organizations 85

status and then convincing men that their support and encouragement is also essential. The basic theme in most official statements regarding the role of women is that women have a responsibility to their families, as well as to their society. Therefore, by enlightening and educating themselves, women are not only helping to raise the status of their entire family, but are also strengthening UAE society in general.[1] And, most importantly, these objectives can be realized by adhering to the requirements of orthodox Islam. Just as Muslim women played a great role in helping to build up Islamic society, so the UAE woman must participate in her own nation's growth, and with no less effort or conviction than that exercised by men. As an example of official policy concerning women, in one of his speeches concerning UAE women, Shaykh Zayid stated that:

I am sure that the Arab women in our reviving country recognize the importance of keeping our genuine customs, which are derived from the teachings of true Islam; and that they know very well that Islam granted them fourteen centuries ago what the women in most advanced countries are trying to get now. Islam has known the importance and true value of women . . . and I call upon my sisters and daughters all over the country to recognize that their responsibilities are great and are not less than those of men in this society. Women in Islamic and Arab history had a great role to play in the building of society . . . For this reason, the nation was great, eminent and proud. Hence we hope that women in the State of the United Arab Emirates will adopt this concept historically; and that they will revive the known glories of the Arab woman. . .[2]

Services Provided by Government Ministries to Improve the Status of Women

The ministry which has the most contacts with women and which is most responsible for providing for their basic needs is the Ministry of Labor and Social Affairs. Within the Ministry, it is the Department of Social Affairs which is involved with women's needs. When it was first established in 1972, the Department of Social Affairs was primarily responsible for distributing aid to 'needy' families.[3] Women who fell into this category were those who were divorced, widowed, or were spinsters, and who had no steady source of income. A woman who never marries need not, therefore, become a burden to her family if they are impoverished. The same holds true for a divorced or widowed woman from a poor family. Remarriage need not be the only solution

86   The Role of Governmental and Non-governmental Organizations

to poverty, as the government now has the means with which to support its less fortunate citizens. Moreover, since 1972, the Ministry's activities have greatly increased beyond primarily distributing welfare benefits and, in the last two years especially, many important innovations have been introduced.

In 1977, the Department of Social Affairs was formally reorganized. Now, according to the UAE Council of Ministers, the prime purpose of the Department of Social Affairs is

> to develop and promote the society within the scope of Islamic and traditional Arab values, and to guard the family, protect children, direct the youth, provide help for the elderly and needy, struggle against social disease, and encourage and support cooperative associations and all associations which benefit the common good.[4]

With this new set of objectives in mind, one of the first innovations of the reformed Department of Social Affairs was the establishment of an experimental women's center in al-Buteen, a suburb of Abu Dhabi. The project was originally organized in conjunction with a staff sent by UNICEF, which helped local authorities determine the needs of the community. The Department of Social Affairs then took over complete control of the project. Female social workers are assigned to visit the aid-receiving families in the Buteen area and explain to them the purpose of the center, which is mainly to provide them with information and lessons in hygiene, child-care, nutrition and education. It is hoped that by acquainting women with modern methods of hygiene, for example, women will apply these methods to their own families, where change must first be made. The center has a doctor and a nurse for all women and children needing medical attention, and the women are encouraged to visit the center on a daily basis to see films and participate in sessions on such topics as first-aid, child-rearing and nutrition. In addition, women are taught cooking, sewing and handicrafts, on a regular basis, once a week. When the facilities are enlarged, in the next year or two, classes will be offered three times a week, as the response to them has been favorable.

The center also offers literacy classes in the morning and, although enrollment is still very limited, fourteen women attend regularly. Without this opportunity to attend classes in the morning, they probably would have remained illiterate as all are mothers of small children and would not be able to leave the children alone at home for long periods of the day. Since the center has nursery facilities, however, there is

The Role of Governmental and Non-governmental Organizations   87

someone to watch the children during the two-hour period that classes in Arabic, math and religion are in session.[5]

Approximately 150 families benefit from the center,[6] although most women do not attend on a daily basis. Rather, anywhere from 15 to 25 women can be found at the center on any of the six days it is open. On special holidays, when parties are organized by the center, greater numbers of women from the area come and participate in the activities. One must also remember that such services are still very new to the local women, and a great effort was exerted initially just to encourage the women to visit the center. One of the greatest problems relating to this is that all of the social workers (seven) associated with the Buteen center are non-local women and therefore many of the local women were at first reluctant to become involved in the center's activities. Now, however, the women in the area have become accustomed to the social workers so there is less hesitancy about visiting the center. The relationship between the center and the community will continue to grow closer because the social workers are assigned to visit every family receiving social aid in the area one time a week and attempt to recruit more regular attendants. The relative success of the Buteen center has been encouraging, and the Department of Social Affairs is now planning to open other such centers throughout the UAE, and especially in the smaller villages since the female residents there are most in need of the services offered by such a center.[7]

Another new project of the Department of Social Affairs is one supervised by the United Nations Development Program, the International Labour Office and UNICEF, which, when open, will be for the benefit of all UAE women, but will be especially oriented to those on social welfare. The plan is to establish an institute for the training of local people in developing local handicrafts. Those women now receiving social aid will be given first priority to develop their skills so that, eventually, they will no longer be dependent on social aid, as they will have an income from the goods they produce. All materials and machinery will initially be provided by the government. The goods produced will then be sold to the government, which will set up shops and sell the products to the general public. It is also hoped that this will encourage more women to come out of their homes and participate in the labor force. Since they will be working only with other women, there should be no conflict with local traditions. At the same time that the women themselves are benefiting from learning new skills, they will also be making an important addition to the local industry which, until now, has had a very small, unorganized handicraft sector.

88 *The Role of Governmental and Non-governmental Organizations*

Another important project of the Department of Social Affairs is the encouragement of the formation of cooperative societies as a form of local organization in which increasing numbers of local people can effectively participate in the economic growth of the community. Co-operatives can be multi-purpose or specialized, and the Ministry of Labor and Social Affairs is willing to provide financial assistance to groups of people (male and female) interested in forming cooperatives. It is hoped that, through such societies, not only will more people develop managerial and business skills, but the community, in general, will benefit through the introduction of new and better-quality consumer products on the market.

Since the Ministry has stressed that men and women are eligible for loans to get cooperatives started, it is not surprising that the first and, to date, the only cooperative, which was formed in Sharjah in early 1977, includes both men and women. The cooperative is composed of a general assembly, which is the supreme body, including all of the shareholders and an executive committee. There are twenty shareholders — male and female. Although all of these people are blood relatives, the situation is still unique because it is the first known business venture where women are actually visible at business meetings, handling financial matters along with the men. The Executive Committee includes eight women and three men, and all are relatively young (late twenties to early thirties). Their goal is to be a multi-purpose cooperative, with branches throughout the Emirates, but at present, because of limited facilities, they are limited to selling household products and food. As the purpose behind such societies becomes more widely understood, it is hoped that more women, as well as men, will be encouraged to become involved because the cooperatives are a form of community service and are similar to work in a government ministry in the sense that one is not working out of personal need but rather for the national good.[8]

In all of its projects, the goal of the Department of Social Affairs is to reach as many women as possible. The sooner women are made aware of the services at their disposal, the faster change will come for their families and for society in general. For this reason, there is very close contact between the Department of Social Affairs and the local women's associations throughout the Emirates. Although the services provided by each organization are different, the goal of each is the same — to increase women's awareness of the changing, increasingly modern world around them, and of the new opportunities available to all. As will be discussed later, the work of the social centers and the women's

The Role of Governmental and Non-governmental Organizations   89

associations will continue to grow closer in the next few years, and all of the newly planned social centers will have a branch of the women's association attached to them.[9]

As we have already seen, the role of the Ministry of Education and Youth in improving the status of women is a prominent one. It is necessary first to cultivate the need and desire for female education, and then to provide the same educational opportunities to males and females, both of which aims are being pursued. Much of the responsibility in these two areas lies with the Social Services Department of the Ministry of Education which organizes parent-teacher conferences to encourage parental enthusiasm in children's education and assigns social workers to tend to the needs and problems of the individual students. On the adult level, female access to education is important not only so that the individual may feel she has gained in status and self-respect, but also because community development is very closely related to eradication of illiteracy among females as well as males. It is therefore vital that the campaigns to end illiteracy be continued. As a United Nations study has shown, it is also essential that the programs be related to practical ends, such as nutrition, child-care, handicrafts and home economics, so as to promote social change at all levels and help women participate in and contribute to, community development.[10] The UAE's Ministry of Education has been diligent in following these recommendations as literacy classes are indeed oriented toward practical goals.[11]

The Ministry of Information and Culture also has an important role to play in improving the status of UAE women, primarily in the field of communications. As one of the first ministries to welcome women into its employee ranks, promoting several of them to positions where women actually have a say in what programs are broadcasted, the Ministry of Information and Culture has shown an interest and willingness in promoting changing attitudes towards women.[12] Through women's access to the media and the official policy of allocating daily radio and television time to present programs on women's issues – on such topics as the availability of special services for women, or the activities of the women's associations – the UAE general public is made aware of the fact that women are independent persons with special needs. Special attention is given to women in the official daily newspapers, *Al-Ittihad* and *Emirates News*, and all women's organizations' activities are reported regularly. The Ministry of Information and Culture thus provides one of the most important services for improving the position and role of women.

90   *The Role of Governmental and Non-governmental Organizations*

Thus, on the official level, it is these three ministries – Labor and Social Affairs, Education and Youth, and Information and Culture – which are most involved in affairs concerning women, and therefore, it is their policies which will strongly determine whether the status of UAE women will improve or not. Up to the present time, each of these ministries has placed women's issues in the forefront, thereby helping to give women the special attention they need and deserve. As long as this policy continues, the role and status of UAE women can only improve.

The Role of Women's Organizations in Improving the Status of Women

Women's organizations, which exist in five of the seven shaykhdoms, are held in high esteem primarily because of the support of the ruling families in each state. And one could even say that the women's associations have been the cause of women's advancement in UAE society rather than its result. Again, the credit for this goes primarily to the efforts of certain ruling families.

The first women's association established in the UAE was the Abu Dhabi Society for the Awakening of Women. After the formation of the union, Shaykha Fatima first began meeting with women in her own state to discuss the role and position of UAE women. Wanting very much to meet the new challenges before them as female members of a modernizing state, and having very little experience to fall back on, it was felt that the first need was for all local women to be made aware of their role in the development process. Women would be introduced, by way of a cultural-type club, to what their role should be in helping the development of their state. The aim of these societies is to create a 'spiritual, cultural and social awakening . . . taking into consideration the nature of women, which is guided by true Arab and Islamic moral values and traditions'.[13] Thus the first women's society was opened in Abu Dhabi in February 1973. Shaykha Fatima then met with groups of women throughout the UAE, and through her efforts, along with those of other female members of ruling families, branches of the women's society were opened in Dubay, Sharjah, 'Ajman and Umm Al-Qaywayn. To strengthen the ties between all of these branches, the Union of UAE Women's Societies was established in Abu Dhabi in August 1975, and monthly meetings are now held between the societies' leaders to co-ordinate activities and report on the progress of each branch.

The organization of each society is basically the same.[14] There is an executive committee composed of the president, vice-president, secretary and treasurer, along with the heads of the various committees

The Role of Governmental and Non-governmental Organizations 91

dealing with religious, social, cultural, health, fine arts, public relations and nursery school affairs. The aim of these committees is to organize activities relating to women in each area, such as inviting lecturers or showing films concerning such topics as women and health, religion, education, as well as providing information on women and women's organizations in other societies.

Formal meetings and lectures are held on a weekly basis and are open to all women in the UAE. Each society also has its day-to-day activities, and, again, any woman is welcome to participate in these activities. There is a library in each chapter with books of law, religion, home economics, science fiction and poetry for use by all members. There are literacy programs in each women's society branch so that those women who cannot attend the Ministry of Education's adult learning centers can attend the program at the women's societies. Here, exactly the same program is followed as in the formal centers; classes in Arabic, arithmetic, and religion are offered during the three hours of scheduled classes held in the afternoon. Daily morning activities include classes in sewing, embroidery, weaving and handicrafts. Annual exhibitions are held by each branch to display the works of the members and to encourage other women to participate in the organizations. Each chapter has also set up nursery school programs, as of 1977, so that more mothers are free to participate in organizational activities. A service is also provided to working mothers with small children.[15]

To acquaint the general public of its purpose and activities, each chapter publishes a monthly magazine with articles on the latest events at the chapters, health-related issues, home-making tips, poetry on Arab women, articles on women's role and famous women in Arab history, and lessons in nutrition, child-rearing and artwork.

Through the Union of UAE Women's Societies, relations with women's organizations and activities outside of the UAE are maintained. Guest lecturers from throughout the Arab world are invited to speak to the local chapters on the role and position of Muslim women in Islamic society, and delegates from the UAE are sent to all major conferences concerning women in the Arab world as well as at an international level.[16]

Although the budgets of the women's organizations were first dependent entirely on personal contributions, now all of the chapters submit annual budgetary requests to the Ministry of Labor and Social Affairs. Thus, their budgets are now partly subsidized by the federal treasury.[17] The women's organizations also recently began working closely with the Minister of Labor and Social Affairs on certain projects. For

92   The Role of Governmental and Non-governmental Organizations

example, the handicrafts center which is to be established in Abu Dhabi by the Ministry of Labor and Social Affairs will be supported by all of the women's societies so as to encourage the project's development. Once it has established itself as an interesting and worthwhile program, it is hoped that other women will be attracted to the handicrafts center. The Department of Social Affairs also urges all of its female welfare recipients to attend the women's societies. The women's social center at al-Buteen often holds joint holiday parties and teas with the Abu Dhabi Women's Society or the Union of UAE Women's Societies to expose the more sheltered women to the services available to them through the women's societies. At present, the Department of Social Affairs is working on setting up a formal committee to coordinate the activities of both the Social Affairs Department and the Union of UAE Women's Societies, and there are already plans that, with the new social services centers to be established throughout the UAE, women's society chapters will be set up alongside them. In the newly formed Bedouin settlements, especially, there is a need for both types of centers since women there have been little, if at all, exposed to modern methods of health care, child-rearing and nutrition. Nor do all of the settlements yet have adult literacy program facilities or places for women to congregate for the purpose of films and lectures, and generally to increase their own awareness of women's new roles and position in other areas of the UAE. So closer ties between the Department of Social Affairs and the women's societies will be to the advantage of all UAE women.

The women's societies also work closely with the Ministry of Education and the local UNICEF office. The Ministry of Education provides the women's organizations with teachers for their literacy programs and offers advice on matters relating to the newly established nursery schools, as does the local UNICEF office. Since UNICEF came into the Gulf area in 1973, it has extended its services to the women's societies, has offered them advice on types of programs to increase women's social participation, has helped train their nursery school teachers and has advised in the purchasing of equipment for the schools.

The very existence of the women's organizations is proof of the success of the women's movement in the United Arab Emirates. Although women did not participate in the early stages of development because they were not accustomed to active participation in community affairs, and while, even now, only 30-60 women attend the daily classes offered in the chapters, greater numbers of local women attend the special lectures and exhibitions. Sometimes as many as 500

The Role of Governmental and Non-governmental Organizations   93

will attend the special events like National Day gatherings or Mother's Day celebrations, where speeches on the role and position of UAE women are always included as part of the programs. It is inevitable that increasing numbers of women will become involved in these societies in the future, especially as more young women become educated and realize the value of the women's organizations. There is an on-going campaign by the women's societies to visit the high schools and explain the purpose of the societies to young girls so that they too will hopefully become active members in the future and be encouraged meanwhile to attend meetings with their mothers.[18] Thus it is likely that, with this new generation, greater numbers of women will actively participate in the women's associations.[19]

The Role of the Ruling Families in Raising the Status of Women

The role of personalities in the Gulf area as a whole is a crucial one, and change for women in most of these states has come about as a result of key figures in the various ruling families. In the United Arab Emirates, where Islamic and tribal traditions are still strongly observed, the impetus, of necessity, had to come from a strong and greatly respected male figure. As fate or luck would have it, the necessary strength and determination were embodied in the character of the UAE head of state and Abu Dhabi's ruler, Shaykh Zayid bin Sultan Al Nuhayyan. Thus it is a strongly held view that without Shaykh Zayid's leadership and support of women's affairs, UAE women would not have received the special attention necessary to bring about an improvement of their role and position. Shaykh Zayid encouraged the idea of a women's society at its inception in 1972, when his wife, Shaykha Fatima, first approached him on the topic. He provided the Abu Dhabi society with a generous budget, a meeting place, automobiles and buses to transport the members, and a professional staff from his private offices to assist in the formalities of setting up such an organization.[20]

Shaykh Zayid now attends most of the major functions of Abu Dhabi's women's society and continues to provide all of the organizations with personal contributions even though the Ministry of Labor and Social Affairs is responsible for providing all of the chapters with an annual budget. Most important of all, his unfailing support of the women's movement in all areas – education, health, employment, and social and cultural organizations – has continued to be expressed within the framework of the tenets of Islam regarding the rights of women; from this derives the public respect for and agreement with his policies concerning UAE women.

94 *The Role of Governmental and Non-governmental Organizations*

As First Lady of the United Arab Emirates, Shaykha Fatima bint Mubarak has achieved great accomplishments through her devotion to improving the role and status of her sisters in the United Arab Emirates. It was she who originally suggested the establishment of a women's society in the UAE, and, on receiving the approval and support of Shaykh Zayid, she has worked tirelessly to improve the status of UAE women. Nor has she limited herself to her position as President of the Abu Dhabi Society for the Awakening of Women, as she is dedicated to women in all areas at all levels throughout the UAE. Shaykha Fatima has been instrumental in founding other women's society chapters in the area and continues to give generous personal contributions to the local chapters – contributions which are used towards increasing their activities or purchasing new equipment. She is also a great supporter of female education and, through her visits to schools of all levels up to and including university, she attempts to instill a love of learning in all UAE females. She is especially concerned that education should reach girls in the remote areas and is supporting the opening of women's societies there, too, so that Bedouin mothers and daughters have all of the educational and cultural facilities of *Hadar* women.

Shaykha Fatima is also a great defender of the employed woman and feels it is the duty of all capable UAE women to work towards building up their society in the public sphere as well as within the family. As for those women who cannot or choose not to work, Shaykha Fatima believes they should receive an education so that they can at least handle day-to-day family problems better. She is a deeply religious woman and also a very traditional one; thus she is sensitive to the constraints on local women, but is also acutely aware that women can become socially active, as Muslim women have been throughout history, without defying Islam or tradition.

Indeed, Shaykha Fatima's dedication to women in general can best be observed through her open, daily *majlis* for women, during which she makes herself accessible to women with grievances or requests. Whether it be a need for urgent medical treatment[21] or a special request for a larger government home, Shaykha Fatima is always ready to listen and provide assistance. Nor is her generosity limited to local women, as Shaykha Fatima's doors are open to foreigners also, and she is always willing to assist towards a good cause. Women residing in the UAE, though not UAE citizens, are also welcome at her *majlis*, and requests or grievances from them are given equal attention.

Shaykha Fatima has been the first ruler's wife in this part of the Gulf to accept invitations for official visits abroad. Again, for the sake of the

The Role of Governmental and Non-governmental Organizations   95

women's issue, and to keep in touch with the functions and activities of other women's societies, Shaykha Fatima has visited Egypt, Morocco and Pakistan. The driving force behind her active concern for women is her strong belief that women cannot be functionless if society is to progress, especially since they comprise one-half of the population and are the builders of families. She and Shaykh Zayid are anxious to see UAE women attain the same level of advancement achieved by women in developed countries, and towards this goal no personal effort has been spared.[22]

In Sharjah, Shaykha Noura bint Sultan Al-Qasimi has also been very much concerned with the issue of women. With the encouragement of her late husband, Shaykh Khalid bin Muhammad Al-Qasimi, Sharjah's former ruler, she established a literacy program for older women in Sharjah before the union was formed, with assistance from the Kuwayt office. She, too, supported the idea of forming women's societies to help raise the consciousness of UAE women about their familial duties and societal obligations, and thus took the leadership role in forming the Women's Society of Sharjah in 1973. Shaykha Noura visits the chapter several times per week and is in charge of all the major decision making. The Sharjah chapter's new facilities, now nearing completion, were financed largely by personal contributions from Shaykha Noura, and her concern for the younger single women in Sharjah prompted the inclusion of a youth club along with the woman's society.

Shaykha Noura is also devout in her religious practices, and she is aware that many of the injustices women have experienced have resulted through human misinterpretations of women's God-given rights. Thus it is her hope that, through the spread of knowledge, more men, as well as women, will become aware of women's true rights so that women can contribute to the building of society. Out of respect for local traditions, however, she feels local women should pursue employment in traditional women's fields such as teaching, medicine or social work since the objective of work is not to raise a woman's personal status, but to help build up the nation. Through her understanding and respect for local traditions, increasing numbers of Sharjah's women have been drawn to the local chapter, and Sharjah's women's society now boasts one of the best attendance records with a range of age groups and social levels being represented.[23]

'Ajman's ruling family has also taken up the cause of women, and Umm 'Ammar, the wife of the Crown Prince, has shown her dedication by heading the women's society of 'Ajman, which was formed in

96   The Role of Governmental and Non-governmental Organizations

1974. Supported by her husband, she became involved in setting up a women's society chapter and now she supervises all the daily activities of the chapter. Umm 'Ammar is also well versed in the Qur'an and extremely religious. In her meetings with women she, too, stresses that it is man who has imposed limits on the role of women, not the Qur'an or Islam. She adds that, if positive change is to come, it must be through strict adherence to the rules of Islam since Islam supports the equality of male and female. Thus, through her example, more women in 'Ajman are becoming involved in social activities, so much so that a new, larger women's society is now being built to house the growing number of members and their projects.[24]

Shaykha Mariam Al-Mu'alla of Umm Al-Qaywayn's ruling family has also supported the establishment of women's societies, and has headed the Umm Al-Qaywayn chapter since its formation in 1972. With teenage daughters of their own, she and her husband, the Minister of Economy and Commerce, have set an example to the community by encouraging their daughters to attend university. Her husband, Shaykh Sultan Al-Mu'alla, has been very supportive of her role in encouraging women to take a more active part in the society. Shaykha Mariam is also deeply religious and well versed in the Islamic rights of women. She believes education to be equally important to females as to males, and during chapter meetings she urges the local women not to push their daughters into marriage before they have had time to finish their schooling. Thus, not only will they be better mothers, but they may also be more useful to their country, which is in need of well-educated citizens. Shaykha Mariam stresses that change will not come until there is an awakening by both men and women as to the value of education. She has noticed an increased awareness of this fact over the past few years as reflected in the growing number of women's society members, but still there is much room for progress. Thus the Umm Al-Qaywayn chapter has also opened up a nursery school to encourage greater enrollment in the society's daily projects. Under the careful supervision of Shaykha Mariam, the Women's Society of Umm Al-Qaywayn has made and continues to make progress toward achieving the goal of awakening women culturally and socially through the variety of activities it makes available to them.[25]

Thus the role of local ruling families is indeed a crucial one in the formation of women's societies. These families not only supply a great deal of moral support to the organizations, but they are equally generous in providing an important source of financial assistance since the government subsidy is not always sufficient. As all of these women

The Role of Governmental and Non-governmental Organizations   97

are working with the full support of their husbands, their example stands as a model for all UAE women to follow. Without their presence, it is doubtful that the women's societies would have come so far in such a short time, or that women's status would have improved so rapidly. By making the issue of women's rights a public one and giving it special attention through the activities of the local women's societies, the process of improving women's status has been hastened.[26]

Conclusion

In improving the status and role of UAE women, non-governmental and governmental organizations have worked as partners since both came into existence in early 1972. Women's organizations, mainly through the active campaigning of prominent women and the support of a progressive leadership, took the first step towards speaking out for women's rights. Certainly, had it not been for Shaykh Zayid's dedication to education and development for all his people, the situation would have been very different for women today. With the rapid spread of educational centers in the late 1960s and early 1970s, the awareness by women's parents of the importance of a good education was also necessary. Women's organizations have taken over the responsibility of broadcasting the importance of education to mothers, and, more importantly, have also brought to the attention of mothers the need for their own education. For, if women are to be part of the quickly changing UAE society, they, too, must develop 'socially and spiritually' so that they can meet their increasing obligations as wives and mothers.

With the support of the heads of the ruling families, collaboration with governmental organizations came automatically. Thus it is primarily the Ministries of Labor and Social Affairs, Education, and Information and Culture which have offered the necessary expertise for forming viable women's organizations. The Department of Social Affairs continues to work closest with women's organizations because of its joint involvement with them on special projects to encourage the increased participation of women in the social development process. The Ministry of Education shares the goal of spreading educational participation along with the women's societies, and its main contribution lies in providing competent training for the teaching staff of the educational programs of the women's organizations. The Ministry of Information and Culture is concerned mainly with broadcasting women's activities. Now with both governmental and non-governmental organizations working towards many of the same objectives, progress

98   *The Role of Governmental and Non-governmental Organizations*

for women has been moving at a faster pace. The establishment of women's organizations brought initial public recognition of the condition of UAE women, and the governmental ministries gave official endorsement of the women's societies' goals, and offered to implement their goals. The result has been an increased awareness and respect for UAE women by both women and men, as well as increased female participation in the overall national development process.

Notes

1. Based on my interviews with officials in the Ministry of Labor and Social Affairs, Education, Information and Culture, and members of ruling families in Abu Dhabi, Sharjah, Umm Al-Qaywayn and 'Ajman.

2. Speech of Shaykh Zayid on the occasion of the founding of the United Arab Emirates' Women's Union in 1975. Reprinted in *The Woman of the United Arab Emirates* (Union of the Women's Societies of the UAE, Abu Dhabi, 1976), p. 2.

3. Abu Dhabi began distributing welfare allowances to its citizens before 1972; then, when the UAE was formed, all needy citizens throughout the seven shaykhdoms were given aid. There are now over 28,000 families receiving aid, according to Ministry sources, and the amount of aid has risen from 7,000,000 dirhams in 1972 to 127,000,000 dirhams in 1977. See 'Social Aid Up', *Emirates News* (April 24, 1978), p. 3.

4. United Arab Emirates, 'Decision of the Council of Ministers on: The Organization of the Ministry of Labor and Social Affairs' (decision released in Abu Dhabi, May 22, 1971), article 1, p. 1.

5. One should also keep in mind that, although there are only 14 women taking literacy classes at the center, women also attend other literacy programs available in the area, offered by the Ministry of Education. Since the center at present only offers the basic literacy program, and not the more advanced levels, it is not unusual that the classes are so small.

6. There are about 300 families in the area, according to Ministry authorities.

7. During my visit a new center was opened in Sharjah, but it was still too early to measure the response of the area women. There are two local women employed as social workers at the Sharjah center, though, so it is likely that it will take less time than it took with the Buteen center to encourage women to visit the Sharjah center and take advantage of its services.

8. Based on my interviews with members of Sharjah's cooperative society and officials at the Ministry of Labor and Social Affairs.

9. Based on my interviews with heads of women's associations and Ministry of Social Affairs officials.

10. United Nations, *Participation of Women In The Community Development* (United Nations Pub., New York, 1972), p. 19.

11. Based on my attendance at several literacy classes and my interviews with female students and teachers.

12. For a discussion on the importance of women's access to the media, see Mallica Vajrathon, 'Toward Liberating Women: A Communication's Perspective' in Irene Tinker and Michele Bramsen (eds), *Women and World Development* (Overseas Development Council, New York, 1976), pp. 95-104.

13. *Nishatat Al-Mar'a* (Abu Dhabi Society for The Awakening of Women, Abu Dhabi, 1975), p. 8.

The Role of Governmental and Non-governmental Organizations 99

14. Based on my interviews with presidents of the societies. Also see ibid., pp. 9-11; The Women's Organization of Sharjah, *Al Mar'a Fi Biladi* (The Arts, Dubay, 1975); and *The Women's Organization of Umm Al Qaywayn* (in Arabic) (Modern Pub., Dubay, 1975).

15. During my stay in the UAE, nursery schools were opened in the Abu Dhabi, Sharjah and 'Ajman chapters of the women's societies and met with great success; several hundred children were enrolled in each school, far more than had been expected, so immediate plans were made for enlarging the new facilities to be built and hiring some additional instructors.

16. The UAE was represented at Mexico for the World Conference of the International Women's Year in 1975 by a delegation of local women headed by Shaykha Moza bint Hilal, assistant to Shaykha Fatima. UAE delegations also attended conferences concerning women in Cairo, Berlin, Damascus, Kuwayt and Morocco, from 1975-77.

17. Even though the women's societies get a large part of their budgets from the federal government, they are still considered independent, non-governmental organizations.

18. An example of this is that, in Shaykha Fatima's most recent speech to female students at the opening of the 1978-79 school year, she asked them to participate in women's activities and said that the women's association is 'open to them and needs their efforts to help build the country'. See 'Her Highness Shaykha Fatima Speaks to Female Students', *Al-Ittihad* (October 11, 1978), p. 2.

19. Saudi Arabia experienced the same problem with low female participation in women's organizations when they were established in new communities in the early 1960s. It was then decided to open clubs for the young girls and approach the mothers through the daughters. Within one year, nearly 1,000 women joined the women's organizations and now meet for two hours a day to discuss community problems, learn reading and writing, sewing, nutrition and other aspects of home economics. See study by Salah Al-'Abd, *Community Development In Saudi Arabia* (United Nations Pub., New York, 1965).

20. The cultural adviser of the *amiri diwan* (The Presidential Court of Advisers) has been authorized by Shaykh Zayid, since 1972, to advise all of the women's societies, through the Union of UAE Women's Societies, on any matters relating to constitutional matters (i.e., helping devise the rules of the societies), providing advice on conferences to be attended, speakers to be invited, and so on.

21. Although medical treatment is free for all UAE citizens, and hundreds are sent abroad each year to receive special treatment that cannot be received at home, sometimes to quicken the process a request to Shaykha Fatima will be made, and the person receives fast, special attention. The same kind of treatment will be given to foreigners in need, and it is not unusual for Shaykha Fatima to receive requests for medical assistance from needy individuals abroad to which she also very often responds positively.

22. Based on my personal observations, having had some ten sessions in the First Lady's *majlis* and meeting with Shaykha Fatima, personally, as well as those women who work closely with her.

23. Based on my several interviews with Shaykha Noura and meetings with members of the Women's Society of Sharjah.

24. A nursery school was opened in December 1977 so that more women could get involved in the society's activities and would not have to worry about the care of their young children. The response was excellent, with over 100 children enrolled and an even longer waiting list. Many of their mothers take sewing and handicraft classes at the society in the morning. This section is based on my interview with Umm 'Ammar and meetings with women at 'Ajman's Women's Society.

100 *The Role of Governmental and Non-governmental Organizations*

25. There are now approximately 100 members of Umm Al Qaywayn's chapter although only 30-40 attend regularly. This section is based on my interview with Shaykha Mariam and members of the chapter.

26. Only the Women's Society of Dubay has no local ruling family member on its executive committee, and it is felt that, mainly because of this, progress has been slower at this chapter. However, Shaykha Fatima has been offering the chapter support since it was formed in 1973 and there is an effort to tie as many of its activities as possible to those of Abu Dhabi's society.

6 CONCLUSION

Although Islam is often criticized for the low status it has assigned to women, a central theme of this study is that it was primarily the interpretations of jurists, local traditions and social trends which caused the status of Muslim women to fall. It is assumed that the law as revealed to the Prophet in fact raised women's status considerably. In the centuries that followed, these laws were reinterpreted to the detriment of women. In the early twentieth century, when the Islamic reform movement arose, one of the major issues put forth by the leaders of this movement was the need to improve the status of women in Muslim society. Thus, over the past fifty years, Muslim women in most parts of the Middle East have been experiencing positive change in their social role and status. However, because of the isolation of the Arabian Gulf region from the Western world, as well as from many of its Eastern neighbors, women and men continued to live by many of their own traditions until recent times. Primarily because of this isolation, modifications in the role and status of both men and women in the Gulf have developed very slowly and very differently from those of people in other parts of the Islamic world. However, with the discovery of oil, the inhabitants of the Arabian Gulf were able to emerge from their seclusion, and positive social and economic change has been realized by all.

The primary objective of this study is, therefore, to examine and assess the contemporary practice of Islamic law in that part of the Gulf known as the United Arab Emirates, in the light of tribal traditions and modernization.

In the first chapter of this dissertation we have attempted to trace the historical development of women's subordinate position in society, in general, and then moved on to discuss the position of women in pre-Islamic Arabia and how, with the advent of Islam, their position improved. In reviewing Suras from the Qur'an, which we rely on as the major determinants of the position of women in Islamic society, it is revealed that women do have rights in situations relating to marriage, divorce, economic independence and education. However, these rights have been violated to a great extent by men who wished to keep women in a subordinate position. We noted in this chapter that, although women's status had greatly deteriorated in most Muslim states

101

102 *Conclusion*

since the early period of Islam, it has recently improved, mainly as a result of the desire for states to 'modernize'.

The position of women in Gulf tribal society has generally been stronger than that of urban, sedentary women in other parts of the Middle East. However, ambiguities still exist when one compares tribal traditions and customs relating to women's status with the rights granted to them under Islamic law. As customs concerning seclusion, payment of *mahr* to the bride, preferential marriages, and divorce, in particular, are not in complete conformity with Islamic law, women in tribal society have not acquired all of their God-given rights. But we have demonstrated that, as all Muslim women have greater access to educational power, they become more aware of their unfair secondary status and attempt to change it.

In the United Arab Emirates, where tribal traditions are still closely observed by the Bedouin as well as the *Hadar*, in the last decade especially these traditions have met head on with the race for modernization. New social values which conflict with the 'old' ways are being introduced in the area. However, the position of women has, for the most part, improved because of the national goals of modernization. In the spheres of marriage and family life, the focus of the second chapter, we find that traditions relating to marriage and the family are in conformity with Islamic laws. Thus there will not be a need for much reform here. Oil wealth has in many cases even strengthened the position of women within the UAE family. Since schooling is now available for all, child marriages are on the decrease as females are delaying marriage until after graduation. Even the terms of marriage are changing as women become less willing to accept unquestioningly any mate their parents choose for them. Polygamy, never widely practiced in the area anyway, is even less resorted to today since fewer people approve of it. Although men can now afford to take on extra wives, the desire to appear 'modern' has led to the increased unpopularity of polygamy. The same holds true for divorce and, although there continues to be no stigma attached to divorced men or women, the 'modern' couple wants a marriage based on mutual understanding and respect, rendering divorce unnecessary. Hopefully, the mate will be one he or she has met and spoken with previously so that less problems related to incompatibility will result. Most important is the fact that none of these new customs contradicts Islamic law regarding family life. Thus the position of women can further improve without violating religious tenets.

We find in the case of female educaton, also, that there is total official agreement with the Islamic law related to equal educational

Conclusion

103

opportunities for all. The UAE government's policy of providing the best available education for all its children, as well as for the adult population, is a commendable one. Therefore, UAE women have not had to fight for this right, as have females in other Muslim Arab states. To increase support for the government's stand, the policy of referring to the Qur'an and providing separate schools for males and females has helped greatly in quieting the objections of some conservatives. For the most part, however, parents who refuse to send their daughters to school are in the minority. Indeed the majority of parents are anxious to have their daughters take advantage of the educational opportunities available so that they may be on a par with women in many of the developed countries they have visited.

Although there are now only two vocational programs for women, in education and nursing, even these have met with little success because of the general attitude which favors university degrees. In the future, hopefully, there will be a greater demand for more varied types of vocational programs so that females can begin to assume jobs in areas where there is a shortage of skilled workers outside of the traditional women's fields.

As economic actors, UAE women have also been limited in their roles, but this is more a result of general economic conditions than of societal pressures to keep them out of the economy. Since women in this area have continued to enjoy rights of inheritance as guaranteed by Islam, unlike women in other parts of the Muslim world, they have a tradition of investing their wealth in business ventures.

The customs of veiling and seclusion have admittedly limited women's involvement in the economy. However, at the same time, they created job openings that only women could fill. Thus, there has always been the need for female teachers, nurses and seamstresses, and these continue to be the favorite jobs of women today. Although Islam views female employment outside of the home as something honorable, local traditions forbidding the public view of women have supported the entrance of women into public sector positions only. When a woman does enter the private sector it is exclusively in the area of business as head of an operation, and she must hire a male to represent her in most business transactions. Undoubtedly, in time, women will branch out into other areas besides the traditional ones for, as they become better educated and aware of their rights, fewer will be hesitant about pursuing such professions as law, journalism or engineering. Since official policy also favors the employment of females, primarily because of the need to lessen the dependency on foreign labor, local women will

104 Conclusion

also be encouraged to forge ahead in non-traditional fields.

The UAE woman has held a relatively high status in her roles as a family person, an educated person and an economically active person, primarily because of strict adherence to Qur'anic law and traditions. Although it may still be too early to judge, it appears that, because of this higher status, UAE women will have a less difficult time in further strengthening their position in society than other Arab women have had. Much of the credit for maintaining this attitude goes to local leaders for their support of women's rights. Through these responsible and knowledgeable leaders, status of women has improved along with that of men. As Rosemarie Said Zahlan has stated: 'The long isolation of the Coast has been lifted completely today. The United Arab Emirates, greatly helped by the income derived from oil, has shown its determination to adapt as quickly as possible to contemporary conditions.'[1]

Note

1. Rosemarie Said Zahlan, *The Origins of the United Arab Emirates* (Macmillan, London, 1978), pp. xvii-xviii.

GLOSSARY

'Abayah – black, cloak-like covering worn by women

Ba'al – husband, lord

Burqu' – mask of canvas, dyed black or purple, covering from the forehead to below the mouth with slits for the eyes

Dinar – ancient gold coin which served as the currency during the Prophet's time

Hadar – settled peoples

Hadith – Prophetic traditions

Harem – female members of the family

Ibn 'Amm – paternal first cousin

Ijma – consensus of the religious authorities on a legal matter

Jahiliyah – pre-Islamic period of ignorance

Kuttabs – schools where Qur'an is taught

Mahr – bride-price

Majlis – conference room; or an informal audience with a ruler's wife in which any local woman can present her problems to the First Lady

Mut'a – temporary marriage; marriage contracted for a specified time and exclusively for the purpose of sexual pleasure

Qadi – judge

Qiyas – deduction by analogy

Riyal – monetary unit formerly used in the shaykhdoms

Shari'a – the law of Islam, as revealed by Muhammad

Shaykh – title of the ruler of any of the shaykhdoms along the Arabian Gulf

Shaykha – title of female member of a ruling family in this area

Sunna – customary procedure, usage sanctioned by practice

Wali – legal guardian

Waqf – transfer of land or houses to a religious organization for perpetual ownership

Zina' – adultery

APPENDIX A

Suras from the Qur'an Relating to Women

The following are selections from the Qur'an[1] which refer to women, primarily, and which have been referred to in the text of the dissertation.

Sura II:177

It is not righteousness that ye turn your faces to the East and the West; but righteous is he who believeth in Allah and the Last Day and the angels and the Scripture and the prophets; and giveth wealth, for love of him, to kinsfolk and to orphans and the needy and the wayfarer and to those who ask, and to set slaves free; and observe proper worship and payeth the poor-due. And those who keep their treaty when they make one, and the patient in tribulation and adversity and time of stress. Such are those who are sincere. Such are the God-fearing.

Sura II:221

Wed not idolatresses till they believe; for lo! a believing bondwoman is better than an idolatress though she please you; and give not your daughters in marriage to idolaters till they believe, for lo! a believing slave is better than an idolator though he please you. These invite unto the Fire, and Allah inviteth unto the Garden, and unto forgiveness by His grace, and expoundeth thus His revelations to mankind that happily they may remember.

Sura II:229

Divorce must be pronounced twice and then (a woman) must be retained in honor or released in kindness. And it is not lawful for you that ye take from women aught of that which he have given them; except (in the case) when both fear that they may not be able to keep within the limits (imposed by) Allah. And if ye fear that they may not be able to keep the limits of Allah, in that case it is not sin for either of them if the woman ransom herself. These are the limits (imposed by) Allah. Transgress them not. For who so transgresseth Allah's limits; such are wrongdoers.

Appendix A 107

Sura II:231

When ye have divorced women, and they have reached their term, then retain them in kindness or release them in kindness. Retain them not to their hurt so that ye transgress (the limits). He who doeth that hath wronged his soul. Make not the revelations of Allah a laughingstock (by your behavior), but remember Allah's grave upon you and that which He hath revealed unto you of the Scripture and of wisdom, whereby He doth exhort you. Observe your duty to Allah and know that Allah is Aware of all things.

Sura II:240

(In the case of) those of you who are about to die and leave behind them wives, they should bequeath unto their wives a provision for the year without turning them out, but if they go out (of their own accord) there is no sin for you in that which they do of themselves within their rights. Allah is Mighty, Wise.

Sura IV:3

And if ye fear that ye will not deal fairly by the orphans, marry of the women, who seem good to you, two or three or four; and if ye fear that ye cannot do justice (to so many) then one (only) or (the captives) that your right hands possess. Thus it is more likely that ye will not do injustice.

Sura IV:4

And give unto the women, (whom ye marry) free gift of their marriage portions; but if they of their own accord remit unto you a part thereof, then ye are welcome to absorb it (in your wealth).

Sura IV:5

Give not unto the foolish (what is in) your (keeping of their) wealth, which Allah hath given you to maintain; but feed and clothe them from it, and speak kindly unto them.

Sura IV:7

Unto the men (of a family) belongeth a share of that which parents and near kindred leave, and unto the women a share of that which parents and near kindred leave, whether it be little or much – a legal share.

Sura IV:11

Allah chargeth you concerning (the provision for) your children; to the

108 *Appendix A*

male the equivalent of the portion of two females, and if there be women more than two, then theirs is two-thirds of the inheritance, and if there be one (only) then the half. And to his parents a sixth of the inheritance, if he have a son; and if have no son and his parents are his heirs, then to his mother appertaineth the third; and if he have brethren, then to his mother appertaineth the sixth, after any legacy he may have bequeathed, or debt (hath been paid). Your parents or your children: Ye know not which of them is nearer unto you in usefulness. It is an injunction from Allah. Lo! Allah is Knower, Wise.

Sura IV:12

And unto you belongeth a half of that which your wives leave, if they have no child; but if they have a child then unto you the fourth of that which they leave, after any legacy they may have bequeathed, or debt (they may have contracted, hath been paid). And unto them belongeth the fourth of that which ye leave if ye have no child, but if he have a child then the eighth of that which ye leave, after any legacy ye may have bequeathed, or debt (ye may have contracted, hath been paid). And if a man or a woman have a distant heir (having left neither parent nor child), and he (or she) have a brother or a sister (only on the mother's side) then to each of them twain (the brother and the sister) the sixth, and if they be more than two, then they shall be sharers in the third, after any legacy that may have been bequeathed or debt (contracted) not injuring (the heirs by willing away more than a third of the heritage) hath been paid. A commandment from Allah. Allah is Knower, Indulgent.

Sura IV:19

O ye who believe! It is not lawful for you to forcibly (to inherit) the women (of your deceased kinsmen), nor (that) yet should put constraint upon them that ye may take away a part of that which ye have given them, unless they be guilty of flagrant lewdness. But consort with them in kindness, for if ye hate them it may happen that ye hate a thing wherein Allah hath placed much good.

Sura IV:20

And if ye wish to exchange one wife for another and ye have given unto one of them a sum of money (however great), take nothing from it. Would ye take it by the way of calumny and open wrong?

Appendix A 109

Sura IV:25

And who so if not able to afford to marry free, believing women, let them marry from the believing maids whom your right hands possess. Allah knoweth best (concerning) your faith. Ye (Proceed) one from another; so wed them by permission of their folk, and give unto them their portions in kindness, they being honest, not debauched nor of loose conduct. And if when they are honorably married they commit lewdness they shall incur the half of the punishment (prescribed) for free women (in that case). This is for him among you who feareth to commit sin. But to have patience would be better for you. Allah is Forgiving, Merciful.

Sura IV:32

And covet not the thing in which Allah hath made some of you excel others. Unto men a fortune from that which they have earned, and unto women a fortune from that which they have earned. (Envy not one another) but ask Allah of His bounty. Lo! Allah is ever Knower of all things.

Sura IV:34

Men are in charge of women, because Allah hath made the one of them to excess the other, and because they spend of their property (for the support of women). So good women are the obedient, guarding in secret that which Allah hath guarded. As for those from whom ye fear rebellion, admonish them and banish them to beds apart, and scourge them. Then if they obey you, seek not a way against them. Lo! Allah is ever High Exalted, Great.

Sura IV:35

And if ye fear a breach between them twain (the man and wife) appoint an arbiter from his folk and an arbiter from her folk. If they desire amendment, Allah will make them of one mind. Lo! Allah is ever Knower, Aware.

Sura V:5

This day are (all) good things made lawful for you. The food of those who have received the Scripture is lawful for you, and your food is lawful for them. And so are the virtuous women of the believers and the virtuous women of those who received the scripture before you (lawful for you) when ye give them their marriage portion and live with them in honor, not in fornication, nor taking them as secret concubines.

110   *Appendix A*

Whose denieth the faith, his work is vain and he will be among the losers in the Hereafter.

Sura VI:151

Say: Come, I will recite unto you that which your Lord hath made a sacred duty for you, that ye ascribe no thing as partner unto Him that ye do good to parents, and that ye slay not your children because of penury – We provide for you and for them – and that ye draw not nigh to lewd things whether open or concealed. And that ye slay not the life which Allah hath made sacred, save in the course of justice. . .

Sura IX:97

The wandering Arabs are more hard in belief and hypocrisy, and more likely to be ignorant of the limits which Allah hath revealed unto His messenger . . .

Sura IX:120

It is not for the townsfolk of Al-Madinah and for those around them of the wandering Arabs to stay behind the messenger of Allah and prefer their lives to his life. . .

Sura XVII:31

Slay not your children, fearing a fall to poverty. We shall provide for them and for you. Lo! the slaying of them is great sin.

Sura XXIV:2

The adulterer and the adulteress, scourge ye each one of them (with) a hundred stripes. And let not pity for the twain withhold you from obedience to Allah, if ye believe in Allah and the Last Day. And let a part of believers witness their punishment.

Sura XXIV:30

Tell the believing men to lower their gaze and be modest. That is purer for them. Lo! Allah is Aware of what they do.

Sura XXIV:31

And tell the believing women to lower their gaze and be modest, and to display of their adornment only that which is apparent, and to draw their veils over their bosoms, and not to reveal their adornment save to their own husbands or fathers or husbands' fathers, or their sons or their husbands' sons, or their brothers or their brothers' sons or sisters'

Appendix A   111

sons, or their women, or their slave, or male attendants who lack vigor, or children who know naught of women's nakedness. And let them not stamp their feet so as to reveal what they hide of their adornment. And turn unto Allah together, O believers, in order that ye may succeed.

Sura XXIV:32

And marry such of you as are solitary and the pious of your slaves and maid-servants. If they be poor, Allah will enrich them of his bounty. Allah is of ample means, Aware.

Sura XXX:21

And of his signs is this: He created for you help-meets from yourselves that ye may find rest in them, and He ordained between you love and mercy. Lo! herein indeed are portents for folk who reflect.

Sura XXXIII:35

Lo! Men who surrender unto Allah, and women who surrender, and men who believe and women who believe, and men who obey and women who obey, and men who speak the truth and women who speak the truth, and men who persevere (in righteousness) and women who persevere, and men who are humble and women who are humble, and men who give alms and women who give alms, and men who fast and women who fast, and men who guard their modesty and women who guard (their modesty), and men who remember Allah much and women who remember — Allah hath prepared for them forgiveness and a vast reward.

Sura XXXIII:59

O Prophet! Tell thy wives and thy daughters and thy women of the believers to draw their cloaks around them (when they go abroad). That will be better, that so they may be recognized and not annoyed. Allah is ever Forgiving, Merciful.

Sura XLVIII:16

Say unto those of the wandering Arabs who were left behind: Ye will be called against a folk of mighty prowess, to fight them until they surrender; and if ye obey, Allah will give you a fair reward; but if ye turn away as ye did turn away before, He will punish you with a painful doom.

112 *Appendix A*

Sura XLIX:13

O mankind! Lo! We have created you male and female, and have made you nations and tribes that ye may know one another. Lo! the noblest of you, in the sight of Allah, is the best in conduct. Lo! Allah is Knower, Aware.

Note

1. *The Glorious Koran*, translated by Marmaduke Pickthall (State University of New York, Albany, 1976).

APPENDIX B

Table 1: Total Enrollment of Male/Female UAE students, 1953-77

		Pupils	
Year	Male	Female	Total
1953-54	230	—	230
1954-55	270	—	270
1955-56	440	30	470
1956-57	580	66	646
1957-58	639	119	758
1958-59	1,954	381	2,335
1959-60	2,491	620	3,111
1960-61	3,194	722	3,916
1961-62	3,861	1,142	5,003
1962-63	4,201	1,293	5,494
1963-64	4,442	1,770	6,212
1964-65	5,244	2,198	7,442
1965-66	6,014	2,823	8,837
1966-67	6,641	4,305	10,946
1967-68	8,253	4,519	12,772
1968-69	11,321	6,544	17,865
1969-70	13,761	8,564	22,325
1970-71	16,850	10,895	27,745
1971-72	21,770	11,092	32,862
1972-73	24,508	15,685	40,193
1973-74	26,154	18,118	44,272
1974-75	30,264	22,057	52,321
1975-76	34,782	27,021	61,803
1976-77	39,300	32,014	71,314

On the basis of available population estimates, there is no way accurately to estimate the percentage of the school-age population that these enrollment figures cover. Most of the expatriate population increase in the past ten years is in the 20-60 age group, but recently the number of people in the foreign population between 5 and 19 has also been greatly increasing so that foreign children now make up 30 percent of the public-school student body (*Educational Abstract, 1976-77*, p. 24). At least 50 percent of the total school-age population is enrolled (Robert Mertz estimated this in 1972, *Education and Manpower*, p. 155) and the actual figure is more than likely much higher than this today because of the spread of education to remote villages and Bedouin settlements since 1972.

Source: UAE Ministry of Education and Youth, *Educational Abstract, 1976-77*, pp. 12-13.

Appendix B: Table 2: Current Budget of the UAE Ministry of Education and Youth 1972-77

Year	1972	1973	1974	1975	1976	1977
Total	62,464,420	122,041,820	186,935,906	346,585,496	569,920,000	888,312,600

Source: UAE Ministry of Education and Youth *Educational Abstract, 1976-77*, p. 5.

Appendix B: Figure 1: Educational Stages in the UAE

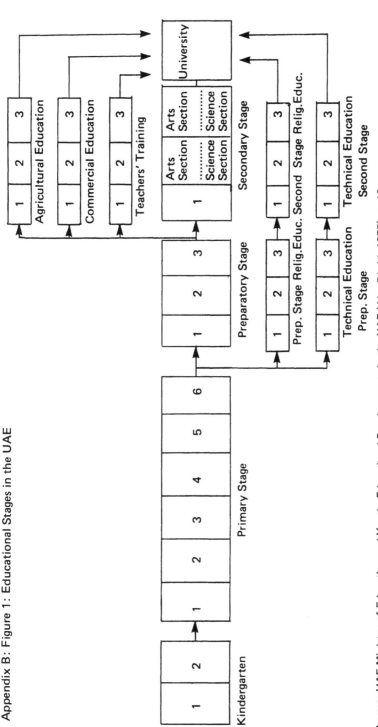

Source: UAE Ministry of Education and Youth, *Educational Developments In the UAE* (Abu Dhabi, 1977), p. 18.

APPENDIX C

Table 1: Employment of Local Women In Government Ministries

Ministry	1973	1974	1975	1977
Education	139	187	218	332
Health/Nurses	—	13	28	—[a]
Social Workers	11	—	14	—[a]
Min. of Interior (Jails, Airport Customs Office)	4	—	10	—[a]
Min. of Information	4	—	12	12
Abu Dhabi National Oil Company	0	0	0	1[b]
Foreign Affairs	0	0	0	2
Electricity and Water	0	0	0	1 (Dubay)
Public Works, Housing and Town Planning	0	0	0	3 (Dubay)

[a]Figures not listed in the *Annual Statistical Abstract* and not available at the time this was submitted.
[b]Figures not listed in the *Annual Statistical Abstract*, but available from the individual ministries.

Sources: For 1973, 1974 and 1975, compilations from an unpublished UN report made of the area; figures for 1977 from the *Annual Statistical Abstract*, pp. 279, 308, 182, 168, 444, 412.

Appendix C: Table 2: UAE Scholarship Students by Specialization and Class 1975-76

Specialization

Class		Arts	Law	Islamic Law	Commerce	Economic & P. Sciences	Sciences	Agriculture	Pharmacy	Engineering	Technology Engineering	Mechanical Engineering	Petroleum Engineering	Electronical Engineering	Electrical Engineering	Medicine	Dentistry	Education	Physical Ed.	Music and F. Arts	Information	Languages	Social Work	Business Adm.	Tech. Inst.	Tel. Communications	Physiotherapy	Marine & Police	Aviation Engin.	Computer	G. Subjects	Total
Orientation or preparatory	M								3	12		2				18	1			5						14				11		66
	F								3	2						7				1												13
St. 1 year University	M	51	18	8	72	21	14	8	4	10						4	4	7	3	17	4		5			23	9	2				284
	F	32	5		3	8	16		2	1						4		6		1		1	3				1					83
2nd Year	M	25	17	5	44	12	4	4		12		2				21		2		6	4		2			4	3	2				169
	F	6			2	3			1							11				2	1		1									27
3rd Year	M	21	14	6	24	12	9	1		7						6		7	1	2	3					1						114
	F	21	2			1	1		1																							26
4th Year	M	17	6	6	13	19	2	1		2						2			1							1						70
	F	5	1																													6
5th Year	M			2						2						5																9
	F															1																1
6th Year	M															1																1
	F																															
Post Graduate	M									1						1	1															3
	F	1					1																									2
Unclassified	M	3	1		19	15			1	44	2	4	1	1	6	13				1		152		29	4	1	1		2	1	2	303
	F	4				3	2									3				2		24					1			2	2	46
	M	117	56	27	172	83	29	14	8	90	2	4	14	1	6	71	6	16	5	31	11	152	7	29	4	44	13	4	13	1	2	1,032
	F	69	8		5	15	20		7	3						26		6		6	1	25	4	5			2			2	2	204
	T	186	64	27	177	98	49	14	15	93	2	4	14	1	6	97	6	22	5	37	12	177	11	34	4	44	15	4	13	3	2	1,236

Source: *Facts and Figures*, p. 51.

BIBLIOGRAPHY

"Aba' Aw la 'Aba'?' *Sawt Al Umma* (Sharjah) (May 22, 1978), p. 8

Abbott, Nabia, 'Woman' in Ruth N. Anshen (ed.), *Mid-East: World Center Yesterday, Today and Tomorrow* (Harper and Brothers Publishers, New York, 1956), pp. 196-212

El-'Abd, Salah, *Community Development in Saudi Arabia* (UN Publication, New York, 1965)

Abdul-Rauf, Muhammed, *The Islamic View of Women and the Family* (Robert Speller and Sons, New York, 1977)

Abu Zahra, Muhammad, 'Family Law' in Majid Khadduri and Herbert Liebesney (eds), *Law In the Middle East* (Middle East Institute, Washington, DC, 1955), pp. 132-78

Albaharna, Husain, *The Arabian Gulf States: Their Legal and Political Status and their International Problems* (Librairie du Liban, Beirut, 1975)

Anderson, Norman, *Law Reform In the Muslim World* (The Athlone Press, London, 1976)

Anthony, John D., *Arab States of the Lower Gulf: People, Politics, Petroleum* (Middle East Institute, Washington, DC, 1975)

'Arab Education Ministers' Meet Opens Today', *Emirates News* (Abu Dhabi, April 18, 1978), p. 1

Aswad, Barbara, 'Social and Ecological Aspects In the Formation of Islam' in Louise E. Sweet (ed.), *Peoples and Cultures of the Middle East*, vol. 1 (The National History Press, Garden City, New York, 1970), pp. 53-74

Baer, Gabriel, *Population and Society In the Arab East* (Praeger, New York, 1964)

Becker, Carl, 'The Expansion of the Saracens' in *The Cambridge Medieval History*, vol. II, Chs XI and XII, pp. 328-90

Bell, Lady (ed.), *The Letters of Gertrude Bell*, vols I and II (Ernest Benn, London, 1977)

Berger, Morroe, *The Arab World* (Doubleday and Co., New York, 1964)

Berque, Jacques, *The Arabs: Their History and Future* (Praeger, New York, 1964)

Boserup, Ester, *Women's Role in Economic Development* (St. Martin's Press, New York, 1970)

—— , *Integration of Women In Development: Why, When, How*

118

Bibliography

(UNDP, New York, May 1975)

Bourguiba, Habib, 'A New Role for Women' in B. Rivlin and Joseph Szyliowicz (eds), *Contemporary Middle East* (Random House, New York, 1965), pp. 352-5

Bullough, Vern L., *The Subordinate Sex* (University of Illinois Press, Urbana, Illinois, 1973)

Carmichael, Joel, *The Shaping of the Arabs: A Study in Ethnic Identity* (Macmillan, London, 1967)

Churchill, Charles W., 'The Arab World' in Raphael Patai (ed.), *Women In the Modern World* (The Free Press, New York, 1967), pp. 106-27

Cole, Donald P., *Nomads of the Nomads: The Al-Murrah Bedouin of the Empty Quarter* (Aldine, Chicago, 1975)

Coulson, Noel J., *Conflicts and Tensions In Islamic Jurisprudence* (The University of Chicago Press, Chicago, 1969)

Cromer, Earl of, *Modern Egypt* (Macmillan and Co., London, 1908)

El-Daghestani, Kazem, 'The Evolution of the Moslem Family in the Middle Eastern Countries' in B. Rivlin and J. Szyliowicz (eds), *Contemporary Middle East* (Random House, New York, 1965), pp. 345-50

Dearden, Ann (ed.), *Arab Women*, Minority Rights Group Report no. 27 (Expedite Graphic Ltd, London, 1975)

Dickson, Harold R., *The Arab of the Desert* (Allen and Unwin, London, 1949)

Doughty, Charles, *Travels In Arabia Deserta* (The University Press, Cambridge, 1971)

'Education: Where Should Money Be Spent?' *Events* (January 13, 1978), p. 39

'Fatima's Call to Girl Students', *Emirates News* (Abu Dhabi, October 11, 1978), p. 3

Fenelon, Kevin, *The UAE: An Economic and Social Survey* (Longman, London, 1976)

Fernea, Elizabeth W., *Guests of the Sheikh; An Ethnography of Iraqi Village Life* (Doubleday and Co., Garden City, New York, 1965)

Fernea, E.W. and Bezirgan, B.Q., *Middle Eastern Muslim Women Speak* (University of Texas Press, Austin, 1977)

Fernea, R.A. and Fernea, E.W., 'Variation In Religious Observance Among Islamic Women' in Nikkie R. Keddie (ed.), *Scholars, Saints and Sufis* (University of California Press, Berkeley, 1972), pp. 385-401

'Focus on Kuwait: Women, An Image of Modernity For Their Gulf Sisters', *International Herald Tribune* (Paris, February 1978), p. 2-S

120 *Bibliography*

'Focus on Saudi Arabia — For Women, Education and Luxury Bring Mixed Blessings', *International Herald Tribune* (Paris, February 1978), p. 10-S

El-Ghannam, Mohammed, *Education In the Arab Region* (UNESCO Pub., Paris, 1971)

Gibb, Hamilton, *Mohammedanism* (Oxford University Press, Oxford, 1970)

Ginsburg, R.B., 'The Status of Women', *American Journal of Comparative Law*, vol. 20, no. 4 (Fall 1972), pp. 585-91

The Glorious Koran, translated by Marmaduke Pickthall (State University of New York, Albany, 1976)

Goode, William J., 'Changing Family Patterns in Arabic Islam', in *World Revolution and Family Patterns* (Free Press, New York, 1963), pp. 87-163

Gordon, David C., *Women of Algeria — An Essay on Change* (Harvard University Press, Cambridge, Mass., 1968)

Halliday, Fred, *Arabia Without Sultans* (Vintage Press, New York, 1975)

Hawley, Donald, *The Trucial States* (Twayne Publishers, New York, 1971)

Hay, Rupert, *The Persian Gulf States* (Middle East Institute, Washington, DC, 1959)

'Her Highness Shaykha Fatima Speaks to Female Students', *Al-Ittihad* (October 11, 1978), p. 2

Hitti, Philip K., *History of the Arabs* (St. Martin's Press, London, 1970)

Holt, P.M., Lambton, A.K. and Lewis, B. (eds), *The Cambridge History of Islam*, vols I and II (The University Press, Cambridge, 1970)

Hourani, Albert, *Arabic Thought In the Liberal Age, 1798-1939* (Oxford University Press, London, 1962)

Houston, Perdita, *Message From The Village* (Epoch B Foundation, New York, 1978)

'How do We Develop Nursing in Our Country?' (in Arabic), *Al-Ittihad* (Abu Dhabi, February 6, 1978), p. 3

International Labor Office, *Equality of Opportunity and Treatment For Women Workers*, Report VIII (ILO, Geneva, 1975)

Jeffery, Arthur, 'The Family In Islam' in Ruth N. Anshen (ed.), *The Family: Its Function and Destiny* (Harper and Brothers, New York, 1949), pp. 39-72

Khadduri, Majid, *Political Trends In The Arab World* (Johns Hopkins University, Baltimore, 1972)

Bibliography 121

——— , *War and Peace In The Law of Islam* (Johns Hopkins Press, Baltimore, 1955)

——— , 'Marriage In Islamic Law: The Modernist Viewpoints' in *The American Journal of Comparative Law*, vol. XXVI, no. 2 (Spring 1978), pp. 213-18

Al-Khalidy, 'Anbara Sallam, *Jaula fil Dhikrayat bayna Lubnan wa Filastin* (Dar Al Nahar Publishing House, Beirut, 1978)

Klein, Viola, *The Feminine Character – History of an Ideology* (Routledge and Kegan Paul, London, 1971)

Leslie, Ann, 'The World's Most Astonishing Women' in *Daily Mail* (London, April 18-May 2, 1975)

Le Tourneau, R., Flory, M. and Duchec, R., 'Revolution In The Maghreb' in P.J. Vatikiotis (ed.), *Revolution in the Middle East* (George Allen and Unwin Ltd, London, 1972), pp. 73-119

Levy, Reuben, *The Social Structure of Islam* (Cambridge University Press, London, 1971)

Lienhardt, P.A., 'Some Social Aspects of the Trucial States' in Derek Hopwood (ed.), *The Arabian Peninsula* (Rowman and Littlefield, New Jersey, 1972), pp. 219-30

Mahmasani, Subhi, 'Transactions In the Shari'a' in Majid Khadduri and Herbert Liebesny (eds), *Law In the Middle East*, vol. 1 (Middle East Institute, Washington, DC, 1955), pp. 179-209

Mansfield, Peter, *The Arabs* (Penguin, London, 1977)

The Women's Organization of Sharjah, *Al Mar'a Fi Biladi* (The Arts Publishing Co., Dubay, 1975)

Mernissi, Fatima, *Beyond the Veil: Male-Female Dynamics in a Modern Muslim Society* (Schenkman Publishing Co., Cambridge, Mass., 1975)

——— , 'The Moslem World: Women Excluded from Development' in Irene Tinker and Michele Bramsen (eds), *Women and World Development* (Overseas Development Council, New York, 1976), pp. 35-44

Mertz, Robert A., *Education and Manpower In the Arabian Gulf* (American Friends of the Middle East Gulf Study, Washington, DC, 1972)

Myrdal, Alva, 'Women Around The World – An Afterword', *The Center Magazine* (May-June 1974), pp. 79-80

Nishatat al-Mar'a (Abu Dhabi Society For The Awakening of Women, Abu Dhabi, 1975)

Nouacer, Khadija, 'The Changing Status of Women and the Employment of Women in Morocco', *International Social Science Journal*, vol. 14, no. 1 (1962), pp. 124-9

122 Bibliography

'Oil Production, Revenues and Economic Development', *The Economist*, QER Special no. 18 (1974)

Patai, Raphael, *Golden River to Golden Road* (University of Pennsylvania Press, Philadelphia, 1967)

Peristiany, J.G., *Honor and Shame: The Values of Mediterranean Society* (University of Chicago Press, Illinois, 1974)

'Persian Gulf Women Find Less Freedom Now', *Christian Science Monitor* (July 2, 1975), p. 1

Phillips, Wendell, *Unknown Oman* (David McKay, New York, 1968)

'Police Department to Employ Women', *Emirates News* (Abu Dhabi, March 20, 1978), p. 1

'Policewomen's Graduation', *Emirates News* (Abu Dhabi, April 18, 1978), p. 1

'President Signs Civil Service Amendment', *Emirates News* (Abu Dhabi, May 27, 1978), p. 1

'Putting Their House In Order', *The Middle East*, no. 48 (October 1978), p. 74

'The Role of Women In Social Reform In Egypt', *The Middle East Journal* (1953), pp. 440-50

Sanger, Richard H., *Arabian Peninsula* (Books for Libraries, New York, 1954)

El Sayed, El Tahry, 'The Working Woman In The Arab Homeland' in *International Women's News* (London), vol. 73, no. 1 (February 1978), pp. 4-5

Schacht, Joseph, 'Pre-Islamic Background And Early Development of Jurisprudence' in Majid Khadduri and Herbert Liebesny (eds), *Law In The Middle East* (The Middle East Institute, Washington, DC, 1955), pp. 28-57

'School Drop-Outs Total 5,038', *Emirates News* (Abu Dhabi, August 19, 1978), p. 3

Sheean, Vincent, *Faisal: The King and His Kingdom* (University Press of Arabia, England, 1975)

Smith, W. Robertson, *Kinship and Marriage In Early Arabia* (The University Press, Cambridge, 1903)

'Social Aid Up', *Emirates News* (Abu Dhabi, April 24, 1978), p. 3

Stark, Freya, *The Southern Gates of Arabia* (E.P. Dutton and Co., New York, 1945)

The Status of Women In Arab Laws In The Light of UN International Conventions (National Council of Lebanese Women, Beirut, 1975)

Stern, Gertrude, *Marriage In Early Islam* (Royal Asiatic Society, London, 1939)

Bibliography

Stiehm, Judith, 'Algerian Women: Honor, Survival and Islamic Socialism' in L.B. Iglitzin and R. Ross (eds), *Women In The World: A Comparative Study* (Clio Books, Santa Barbara, California, 1976), pp. 229-41

Taki, Ali, *The Changing Status of The Bahraini Women* (Oriental Press, Bahrayn, 1974)

'Ten Years of Women's Lib', *Sunday Times* (London), Special Supplement (October 1, 1978), pp. 27-58

Thesiger, Wilfred, *Arabian Sands* (E.P. Dutton and Co., New York, 1959)

United Arab Emirates, Ministry of Education and Youth, *Educational Abstract, 1976-1977* (Abu Dhabi, 1978)

——, Ministry of Education and Youth, *Educational Developments In the UAE* (Abu Dhabi, 1977)

——, Ministry of Education and Youth, *Annual Report of the Social Services Dept., 1975-1976* (in Arabic) (Abu Dhabi, 1977)

——, 'Decision of the Council of Ministers on: The Organization of the Ministry of Labor and Social Affairs' (decision released in Abu Dhabi, May 22, 1977)

——, Ministry of Information and Culture, *Facts and Figures* (Zug, Switzerland, 1976)

——, Ministry of Planning. *Annual Statistical Abstract, 1972-1976* (Abu Dhabi, 1977)

United Nations, *Demographic Yearbook, 1971* (UN Publication, New York, 1971)

——, *Participation of Women In Community Development* (UN, New York, 1972)

——, *Participation of Women In The Economic and Social Development of Their Countries* (UN, New York, 1970)

——, *Report of the Interregional Meeting of Experts on the Integration of Women in Development* (UN, New York, 1973)

——, *Status of Women and Family Planning* (UN, New York, 1975)

United Nations, UNESCO, *Report on The Relationship Between Educational Opportunities and Employment Opportunities for Women* (Paris, July 20, 1975)

'University A Pillar of Unity', *Emirates News* (Abu Dhabi, October 16, 1978), p. 3

Vajrathon, Mallica, 'Toward Liberating Women: A Communications Perspective' in Irene Tinker and Michele Bramsen (eds), *Women and World Development* (Overseas Development Council, New York, 1976) pp. 95-104

124 Bibliography

Vernier, Pierre, 'Education for Arab Girls, Economic Expansion, Changing Attitudes Favour Progress', *UNESCO Features*, no. 437 (April 1964), pp. 14-17

Vesey-Fitzgerald, S.G. 'Nature and Sources of The Shari'a' in Majid Khadduri and Herbert Liebesny (eds), *Law In The Middle East* (The Middle East Institute, Washington, DC, 1955), pp. 85-113

Von Grunebaum, Gustave E., *Medieval Islam* (University of Chicago Press, Chicago, 1969)

Watt, H. Montgomery, *Muhammad: Prophet and Statesman* (Oxford University Press, Oxford, 1969)

'Who Will Buy My Sweet Daughter?', *The Middle East* (August 1978), pp. 58-9

Winder, R. Bayly, *Saudi Arabia In the 19th Century* (Macmillan and Co., London, 1965)

The Women of the United Arab Emirates (Union of the Women's Societies of the UAE, Abu Dhabi, 1976)

'Women In US Slowly Entering "Male" Fields', *International Herald Tribune* (Paris, June 5, 1978), p. 5

'Women Police End Course', *Emirates News* (July 27, 1978), p. 3

'Women's Lib-Kuwait Style', *The Middle East* (May 1978), pp. 78-83

The Women's Organization of Umm Al Qaywayn (in Arabic) (Modern Publishing Co., Dubay, 1975)

Woodsmall, Ruth F., *Eastern Women Today and Tomorrow* (Central Committee On The United Study of Foreign Missions, Boston, 1933)

—— , *Moslem Women Enter a New World* (G. Allen and Unwin, London, 1936)

—— , *Women and The New East* (Middle East Institute, Washington, DC, 1960)

Youssef, Nadia H., 'Women In The Muslim World' in L.B. Iglitzin and R. Ross (eds), *Women In the World: A Comparative Study* (Clio Books, Santa Barbara, California, 1976), pp. 203-17

—— , 'Women In World Development: Urban Life and Labor' in Irene Tinker and Michele Bramsen (eds), *Women and World Development* (Overseas Development Council, New York, 1976), pp. 70-7

—— , *Women and Work In Developing Societies*, Population Monograph Series, no. 15 (University of California, Institute of International Studies, Berkeley, 1974)

Yusuf, Shaykh Hajii, 'In Defense of the Veil' in B. Rivlin and J. Szyliowicz (eds), *The Contemporary Middle East* (Random House, New York, 1965) pp. 355-9

Bibliography

Zahlan, Rosemarie Said, *The Origins of the United Arab Emirates* (Macmillan, London, 1978)

INDEX

'abayah 32, 37-8
Abu Dhabi Society for the
Awakening of Women 90, 94
ambition, personal 41, 48n

Bedouin, the 11, 17-20, 31, 36, 37,
94, 102
broadcasting 73-4, 89
burqu' 32, 37-8
Buteen center 86-7

clubs, women's 45
complementarity 15
cooperative societies 88

divorce 17, 19-20, 29, 30, 43-4, 102
doctors 72
dowry *see mahr*

earnings, control of 79
economic roles *see* employment
education 49-65, 94, 102-3; adult
58-60, 65n; budget 114;
curriculum 54; incentives to 52;
parents and 53-4; significance of
21-2; spending on 61-2; stages in
UAE 115; traditional 95; vocational 55-6, *see also* literacy
employment 22, 66-83; as sales-
girls 76; clerical 71, 74-5;
domestic work 36, 75; in government ministries 116; motivation
and 78, 80; private sector 75-7,
103; professional 58, 69, 75, 103;
public sector 67, 70; rights 77;
skilled workers shortage 103;
traditional 67, 68-9
equal pay 77
equality, sexual 15
expatriate labor 76, 83n, 84
extra-marital relationships 17

family, the 102; activities 38-9;
bride's place in 34-9; children in
39-42; employment and 77-9,
82-3n; size 40; structure of 21,
22
Fatima, Shaykha 52, 59-60, 61, 63n,

90, 93-5, 100n
friendship 39

glossary 105
governmental organizations 85-90

Hadar, the 11, 102
Hadith, the 14, 49
handicrafts 87, 92
harem 32
honor 18, 19; work and 69

Industrial Revolution 9
infanticide 13
inheritance 17, 66, 79, 103
investment 76-7
Islam 101; education and 49-50;
teaching of 41
Islamic law 9-10, 11, 101-2; marriage
and 28-30; women under 14-17

Khalid bin Muhammad Al-Qasimi,
Shaykh 95

labor legislation 77
leisure 36-7
liberation 9, 83; men's reaction to
23
literacy 21, 49, 58-60; organization
and 86-7, 89, 91, 98n; rates 62n

mahr 19, 20, 28, 32, 33, 43, 66; cost
of 33-4
Mariam Al-Mu'alla, Shaykha 96
marriage 28-48, 102; age at 32-3;
arrangement procedure 31-3;
children's rights 29-30; contract
28; delayed 78-9; husband-wife
relationship 35-6; personal choice
and 47n; pre-Islamic 13-17;
remarriage 19, 28-9, 44; rules for
16-17; selection of partner 20,
23, 28, 30-4; to first cousins 19,
30, 31; to non-Muslims 29; *Wali*
28
matrilineage 13, 20
medical treatment 99
middle classes 83n

126

Index

Ministry of Education 51, 74, 92, 97;
    Department of Social Affairs
    85-9, 97; Social Services Depart-
    ment 89
Ministry of Foreign Affairs 75
Ministry of Information and Culture
    74, 89, 97
Ministry of Justice 75
Ministry of Labor and Social Affairs
    71-2, 85, 91-2, 97
Ministry of the Interior 74
modernization 20-4, 102; education
    and 60; effects of 23; employ-
    ment and 67
mosques 15
Moza bint Hilal, Shaykha 60
Muhammad (the Prophet) 14, 28, 53,
    66
Muhammad Ibn 'Abd Al-Wahhab 18

nationalism 21
newspapers 89
non-governmental organizations 90-3
Noura bint Sultan Al-Qasimi,
    Shaykha 95
nursing 72-3, 82n
nursing school 55-6, 64n, 72-3

oil wealth 11, 30, 84, 101, 102

patrilineage 13, 18, 20
pearling 68
police force 74
polyandry 13
polygamy 16, 29, 30, 40, 42, 102
population control 22, 40, 78
poverty 85-6
property 17, 29
puberty 19

Qasim Amin 50
Qur'an, the 9, 13-18, 20, 39, 49, 70,
    101, 104; Suras from relating to
    women 106-12

ruling families 31, 52, 53, 93-7

schools 50-5; drop-outs 53, 56, 63n,
    65n; enrollment 63n, 64n, 113;
    nursery 96, 99n; private 51; segre-
    gation of 54-5, 62; technical 51
sex segregation 71, 76, 81
single women 44-6
social work 71, 87

stability 46-7
status 18, 80
Sultan Al-Mu'alla, Shaykh 96

teacher training 55-6
teachers 63n, 70-1
tribal traditions 12, 17-20, 102

UNICEF 87, 92
Umm 'Ammar 95-6
Union of UAE Women's Societies 90,
    92
universities 51, 56-8, 64n, 117

values 46
veiling 14, 19, 21, 37-8, 103; origin
    of 15-16

waqf 66
welfare provision 44, 85, 98
Western influences 22
widowhood 44
women: economic role 79-80;
    political role 23; pre-Islamic
    position 13
women's associations 88, 90-3, 99n

Zayid bin Sultan Al Nuhayyan,
    Shaykh 52, 57, 59-60, 61, 63n,
    69, 70, 85

CPSIA information can be obtained
at www.ICGtesting.com
Printed in the USA
BVHW06s1415280918
528719BV00010B/129/P